INTERESTING WAYS TO TEACH

53 Problems
with large classes
Making the best of a bad job

53 Problems
with large classes
Making the best of a bad job

Sue Habeshaw
Senior Lecturer and Course Adviser
University of the West of England, Bristol

Graham Gibbs
Head, Oxford Centre for Staff Development
Oxford Brookes University

Trevor Habeshaw
Educational Consultant
TES Associates, Bristol

First published in 1992 by
Technical and Educational Services Ltd.
37 Ravenswood Road
Bristol BS6 6BW
U.K.

ISBN 0 947885 70 6

Printed in Great Britain by BPCC Wheatons Ltd., Exeter, U.K.

Books from Technical & Educational Services

Preparing to teach: *An introduction to effective teaching in higher education*
53 Interesting things to do in your lectures
53 Interesting things to do in your seminars and tutorials
53 Interesting ways to assess your students
53 Interesting ways of helping your students to study
53 Interesting communication exercises for science students
53 Interesting ways to appraise your teaching
53 Interesting ways to promote equal opportunities in education
53 Interesting ways to teach mathematics
53 Interesting ways to write open learning materials
253 Ideas for your teaching
Interesting ways to teach: *7 Do-it-yourself training exercises*
Creating a teaching profile
Getting the most from your data: *Practical ideas on how to analyse qualitative data*
Writing study guides
Improving the quality of student learning
53 Problems with large classes: *Making the best of a bad job*

Acknowledgements

We wish to thank these friends for their help and support
in the publication of this book

Jo Corke
Jackie Lublin
Pete Rogers
Adrian Shaw
Jenny Walters

Preface

Our policies are designed to ensure that higher education continues to expand efficiently alongside improvements in quality. When we came into office only one in eight of the relevant age group went into higher education. Now it is one in five. By the end of this decade, we expect one in three of all young people to benefit from higher education of our traditional high quality.

Kenneth Clarke, Secretary of State for Education, House of Commons, 20 May 1991

In higher education we are certainly experiencing the continuing expansion in student numbers predicted by Kenneth Clarke. Indeed, some civil servants involved in the planning and management of change in U.K. higher education have concluded that the expectation referred to by the Secretary of State had been substantially achieved, though unplanned, by the recruitment of new students into higher education for the 1992-93 session. If we are not experiencing the corresponding improvements in quality this is not due to lack of commitment on the part of staff, most of whom welcome in principle the broadening of educational opportunities. Deterioration in standards has occurred because of inadequate preparatory building programmes, a lack of financial provision to cater for the extra students (especially the failure to enhance library provision), and lack of time and training to help staff adjust to the rapid changes.

This book is written for staff who are trying to cope with this difficult and stressful situation.

Readers familiar with the *Interesting Ways to Teach* series will know that we characteristically adopt a positive attitude and focus on interesting ideas rather than problems. This book is rather different. Because it has been written as a response to the many problems which higher education staff face when teaching large classes, we have made the problem the focus of each of the fifty-three items before offering solutions.

The solutions we offer are of three different kinds. Some problems can be solved by the introduction of a change in teaching and learning which is good educational practice, irrespective of the size of group. An example of this is self and peer assessment by students (items 51 and 52). We find a certain irony in the fact that we have for years been among those keen to promote this method of assessment but on the grounds that it is educationally and ideologically sound rather than as a response to financial constraints. Other problems can be handled by practices which, while not being ideal, may be the best solutions available to you in the circumstances: making video-recordings of lectures, for example (item 16). In the case of the third group of problems, where staff are being asked to implement procedures which are oppressive, and alienating and unjust, our advice to you is to resist. Legitimate and practical ways of doing this in an institutional context are suggested in item 14.

We believe that some of the best characteristics of British higher education have already been destroyed by the shortsightedness of government policies, the self-interested compliance of much institutional management and the weakness and apathy of many teachers and their leaders.

It is the purpose of this book to encourage those who feel as we do to hold on to those educational principles and practices which are right for our students.

Sue Habeshaw
Graham Gibbs
Trevor Habeshaw

Bristol 1992

Contents   Page

Chapter 1

The course

1 Some of the students shouldn't be in higher education
2 It's impossible to interview all the applicants
3 Staff can't meet all the needs of new students
4 Students don't have the information they need
5 It's difficult to keep track of everything
6 There isn't time to meet all the course objectives
7 Large groups are too heterogeneous
8 There aren't enough books in the library
9 Students easily become socially isolated
10 Students don't feel involved with the course
11 Students don't get the individual help they need
12 Students don't have independent learning skills
13 Students don't feel valued
14 Staff feel powerless

Some of the students shouldn't be in higher education   1

Some of your students are not yet ready to undertake a course in higher education. Others are not suited to studying. Yet others have been persuaded to apply by parents or teachers but are not really interested. Some enrol because they prefer higher education to unemployment, and for others yours may simply be the wrong course. These students risk the painful experience of withdrawal or failure. The students who shouldn't be there are also the students most likely to make demands on staff time. You are doing everyone a favour if you dissuade them from coming to university, especially when, as today, there are plenty of other suitable and motivated applicants.

You can do this in several ways.

Advertising your course
Advertise your course in an honest way that makes it clear what it is really like and what demands it makes on students. If your department has open days, you have a chance to reinforce the message. For example, if you favour independent learning, you will want to discourage students who are likely to be dependent and are antipathetic to such methods.

Sifting applications
When assessing application forms, read very carefully between the lines of the applicant's personal statement and the referee's letter, looking for signs of limited enthusiasm and commitment. As an exercise to develop your sensitivity to hidden messages, you and your colleagues could re-read the application forms of those students who failed or withdrew last year and compare them with those of some of your more successful students.

Pre-testing applicants
There are some parts of your course which students find more difficult than others and which act as a filter, collecting up those students who are out of their depth and who will take up a large amount of staff time. You can pre-

test applicants on these difficult areas to check on their prerequisite knowledge or skills and turn away those who fail the test. Refer them to preparatory or prerequisite courses or remedial material and invite them to reapply later.

It's impossible to interview all the applicants 2

The admission interview serves two main purposes: it gives staff the opportunity to decide whether they want to offer the applicant a place and it gives applicants the opportunity to decide whether in fact they want the place.

On some large degree courses nowadays, where the entry criteria are a specific number of points at A-level and a favourable reference from the applicant's school, many applicants are offered places without an interview. Other applicants do still need to be interviewed, however, particularly those who come by the access or non-standard entry route, or who have disabilities. Groups of staff may also have their own particular reasons for preferring to interview: for example staff who are preparing their students for a career in the caring professions and who feel they have responsibilities to the students' future clients.

With increasing numbers of places on courses and of applications for those places, it is becoming impossible to conduct all the interviews on an individual basis. Some alternatives are suggested here.

Group information sessions
Much of what goes on in individual admission interviews tends to be repetitive: staff give the same information to everybody, applicants ask the same questions and staff give the same answers. A way of saving time here is to begin with an information and question session for all candidates, followed by individual interviews.

Group admission interviews
If you hold group interviews, not only do you save more staff time but also you gain an insight into how applicants conduct themselves in a group and cope with the dynamics.

A suitable number of applicants for a group interview is about six to eight.

You will need two interviewers so that at any given moment one is running the interview and the other is observing and making notes. You may also wish to involve a student who is currently on the course. A suggested format for a 45-minute interview follows.

a   Explain the interview format to the applicants and your rationale for working in this way. Assure them that they will in addition be offered the option of an individual interview at the end.

b   Begin with a round in which each applicant in turn answers a general question such as 'Would you like to say something about yourself?' or 'Why do you want to do this course?' or 'What experience have you had in this area?' Allow a few minutes for each applicant to speak.

c   This can be followed by further questions to individuals, either from the interviewers or from other applicants. With some groups, this can develop into a discussion.

d   Take some time to give the applicants any information about the institution and the course which you want them to have.

e   Invite the applicants to ask questions.

f   Ask whether anyone would like an individual interview. (This offer is likely to be taken up only by applicants with special circumstances such as a disability or problems with child care arrangements.)

g   Close the interview and discuss the applicants.

Staff can't meet all the needs of new students 3

New students have a whole range of different and urgent needs. It can be an overwhelming experience for staff to try to meet these needs, particularly with large numbers of students. Support offered by staff can, however, be supplemented by support from established students on the same course, who will be able to help in special ways since they have recent experience of being new students on the course and see things from a student's point of view.

Student-led induction

Induction is a painful experience for most new students. They often feel overwhelmed, confused, anxious and homesick. It is in this state of mind that they are introduced to the institution and its procedures and on many courses are required to make important decisions about module choice etc. They find it very reassuring if they are welcomed into a small group by a current student who answers their questions sympathetically and explains to them the mysteries of the course from a student's point of view.

If you want to have student-led groups in your induction programme you will need to set up the situation by asking for volunteers at the end of the previous academic year. (Clearly, the more volunteers you enlist, the smaller the groups can be.) You should hold a briefing meeting for volunteers shortly before induction, in which you can rehearse the information that the student helpers need to give to the new students, organise the groups and allocate roles: you may, for example, want to identify students who will be responsible for answering queries about particular subject areas, crèche facilities or accommodation in halls. You should hold another meeting after induction to ask the volunteers for their feedback and to thank them for their help.

Special interest groups

There may be groups of students on your course who feel oppressed because they are in a minority. These may be mature students, or access students or lesbians and gays or students with particular religious or political affiliations. If they have already formed such a group, you could encourage them to make themselves known at induction and welcome new students to join them. If they have not already formed a group, you could help them to do so.

Peer pairing

Peer pairs are pairs of students, one new and one established (usually from the second year), who are paired so that the established student can help the new student to settle in to university life and get the most out of the course. If you want to set this up you will need to speak to your second year students, explain the system and enlist their help. You should also reassure them as to the limits of their responsibility for the new student. Once the system is in train, all that is required from staff is the organisation of the pairing itself; students will need very little briefing because they will simply pass on the kind of support which they themselves received.

Study skills

Most students on study skills courses are in their first year. But occasionally second year students will come to a session when they find they need help. First year students seize the opportunity to ply a second year with such questions as 'Did you find the first year difficult too?...So you got through the exams O.K., then?...But did you panic?' The second year student will, often unwittingly, give the group as much study skills support as the tutor would have done.

If this situation does not arise in your study skills class, you could set it up by encouraging some of your second year students to attend. If the group is large, you could set students to work in mixed sub-groups.

Proctoring

Proctoring is formal teaching of less advanced students by those who are more advanced. In science, postgraduate students are often paid to assist lecturers in large problem-solving classes though this practice is not widespread in other discipline areas. It remains a proposition with a lot of potential because both groups, those teaching as well as those being taught, are likely to gain so much from the experience. Proctoring is well established in the U.S.A. where sophomores are paid, for example, to work in the library and help freshmen learn to use the catalogue.

Experienced students

If you have a group of students who are about to embark on a new phase of their course, like a work placement or a set of specialist options, you can invite students who have already had this experience to come and talk to your group.

Students don't have the information they need 4

In small classes, teachers spend a lot of time giving students information about the layout of the university, the structure of the course, the system of assessment and so on. Without proper documentation, they find themselves responding to numerous individual requests for clarification. In large classes, it is not possible to respond to such requests and there are few opportunities for informal questioning by students. As a result, students fail to get the information they need. This makes them less likely to do well on the course and also makes them feel confused and alienated.

Student handbook
In order to give students the information and reassurance they need, you should write a comprehensive course guide or student handbook and give a copy to every student (and also to your colleagues). You will need to impress upon them the need to read it carefully and to refer to it whenever they need information.

Below are some suggestions for items you may want to include in such a handbook. It is also a good idea to invite student representatives to help you with your handbook, so that you do not omit anything important.

- A map of the institution showing the location of the refectory, the library, the departmental office, lavatories, teaching rooms, student and staff pigeon holes, course noticeboard etc.

- A list of the names and room numbers of important people: the departmental secretary, year tutors, course leader, head of department etc.

- A list of the room numbers, telephone numbers and opening hours of services available to students: accommodation, counselling, careers, computer rooms, Students' Union etc.

- A course calendar for the year indicating dates of union meetings, course management meetings, bank holidays etc.

- Aims of the course.

- An overview of the course, with descriptions of modules or other course elements.

- A copy of the weekly timetable.

- Full details of short courses available to students: study skills, word processing, careers etc.

- A calendar of deadlines for all assessed work, with details of the procedure for submitting assignments and applying for extensions.

- A set of criteria for assessment.

- Extracts from the examination regulations, giving information on how the final result is computed, how students can appeal, and what they should do if they are ill or affected by other extenuating circumstances.

It's difficult to keep track of everything 5

Larger numbers of students bring with them organisational problems. The lines of communication are lengthening each year. In order to be able to keep track of everything on your course you will need to tighten up your procedures as student numbers increase.

Systematise procedures
Analyse and evaluate your procedures for planning courses, organising teaching, allocating responsibilities, supporting and assessing students, keeping records etc. Make sure that you have an efficient procedure for everything and ensure that all staff and students are informed of these procedures.

Computerise procedures
With large numbers of students it is economic, as well as efficient, to computerise all standard procedures, such as the collating of assessment marks. Spreadsheets are ideal for this: they can cope with complex weighting systems and enable customised print-outs to be provided for different groups, such as students and examiners.

Design forms
The use of forms standardises practice and simplifies record keeping. You can design NCR forms to be used as:
    receipts for coursework
    authorisations for assignment extensions
    records of project supervision sessions
    assignment attachment forms (see item 48)
    records of continuous assessment marks.

Write form letters
Use a personal computer to write form letters and other standard documents (notices, handouts, reminders etc.) which you produce each year. It helps if you develop an efficient retrieval system and if you and your colleagues have

personal computers capable of running the same software so that you can exchange records easily as the course progresses.

Record decisions

Use the wordprocessing functions of the computer to write formal minutes for meetings of the course team so that there is a record of decisions that are taken. It may not be necessary for everyone to have a hard copy of the minutes but, if all colleagues have the same computer equipment, they will have a copy on disk to refer to.

There isn't time to meet all the course objectives 6

Courses which were designed for a target group of a particular size are not going to be appropriate for a much larger group, where there is less time available, less support for students and where communication is more difficult. As your student numbers increase, you and your colleagues will probably find that it becomes unrealistic to try to meet your former course objectives.

Reduce course objectives

What is then needed, upsetting though this may be, is a severe pruning of your expectations so that you can concentrate on the really important aspects of the course. You can identify these by asking yourselves some key questions.

If you have ever found yourselves saying at an exam board or planning meeting, 'You can't let a student graduate who can't do x' this should give you a starting point. Ask yourselves what x is. Should a student have a degree in ecology without having done some outside fieldwork? Or a degree in botany without being able to identify *Rubus Fruticosus*? Or in literature without having studied critical theory?

Other questions which you can ask yourselves include:
What do we want students to learn from this course?
To what extent does the course achieve this?
And where does it fall short?
What will we need to do in order to redesign the course?
What is it about the course that we most cherish?

Once you have identified the parts of the course which you intend to protect, everything else can be more or less negotiable in a process of choice and elimination.

It may not only be in the area of objectives that you have expectations of your course which are unrealistic and where you need to sort out your priorities. You may want to do a similar exercise with, for example, the student experience or staff conditions of service.

Large groups are too heterogeneous 7

Many courses with small student numbers have a teaching programme which is tailor-made for them, with lectures aimed specifically at their needs. This means that, for example, an epidemiology lecturer may give lectures on epidemiology for nurses, epidemiology for health visitors and epidemiology for doctors, which he or she will illustrate with different examples depending on the particular disciplines of each student group. Similarly, a research methodology lecturer may give differently focussed lectures on a range of courses in a science department.

Where staff are obliged to operate economies of scale, students from the range of discipline areas are timetabled in one room at one time and taught as one group. The subject of the lecture is then epidemiology, or research methodology, with no concessions to the requirements of the particular student groups.

Make specific connections

If you are put into this situation you have no choice but to limit your lectures to the core material of your subject area. You will have to count on the students to make connections for themselves and apply the lecture material to their own disciplines. There are various ways in which you can help them to do this.

• If the students have set texts which were chosen because of their relevance to their occupation, e.g. *Physiology for nurses*, or *Psychology for social workers*, you can look through these texts for opportunities to make appropriate connections with your own lectures.

• You can schedule breaks into the lecture where you ask students to think of examples from their own discipline areas to illustrate what you have been saying. They can either discuss these in small cognate groups or note them down to discuss later in seminars.

- Seminars or workshops which follow lectures can be run by tutors from different discipline areas so that they can provide examples of applications to their own discipline of each new theory or principle.

- You can set tests with a mixture of general theoretical and discipline-specific questions.

- You can ask students questions in discussion groups or exams which require them to apply to their own disciplines the principles which they have been taught in the lectures, e.g. 'Assess the relevance of a study of epidemiology to the work of a nurse/health visitor/doctor'.

There aren't enough books in the library 8

Every educational library is facing the problem of being unable to provide enough copies of the recommended books to cater for increasing numbers of students.

If a tutor gives a class a reading list, only a small proportion of the students will be able to get hold of the books and read them. Nor does buying duplicates of key texts solve the problem: library funds will never catch up with student numbers and most institutions have stopped trying to meet this increasing demand. There are, however, solutions to this problem which do not entail too much expenditure.

Broaden the scope of your assignments

When you set assignments, try to cover a wide range of topics or at least material which is available in a number of different books. The broader the scope, the larger the number of students who will be able to find library books to help them with their assignments.

Place books on short loan

If library loans are shorter, more students can read each book. The books on your reading list can be placed on short loan immediately before they are required and go back into general use when that part of the course is over. Your reading lists should indicate the period during which particular books will be placed on short loan.

Use resource boxes

Some librarians also operate a short loan system based on course-specific resource boxes. You can put together a box of photocopies of newspaper and journal articles, chapters from books, videos and other materials relevant to your course which the students can borrow on short loan. You will need to ask the librarian of your institution for advice on copyright.

Set up learning teams

Set up learning teams of students who share books and pool information on alternatives to books on the reading list.

Abandon the reading list

The idea of key texts is constructed by tutors. Since there are in fact thousands of books in educational libraries and not enough multiple copies of the key texts, one answer is to abandon the reading list. Librarians often comment that students will search for a particular book and leave the library empty-handed even though the shelves are full of books which contain very similar material.

If, instead of giving your students a reading list, you tell them 'Go to the library and see what you can find', this will be a real learning task and one which will result in variety and richness: a group of students who have all read different material will produce a much more interesting discussion from their multiple viewpoints than a group restricted to a few texts.

Create your own reader

If there are particular articles and chapters or other sections from books that you require your students to read, the only way to ensure that they all get access to a copy is to give them one.

You can create your own reader by photocopying the required material and getting your reprographic unit to bind it for you. If your department cannot afford to fund the printing of these readers you may have to sell them to students. Students will think this is worthwhile if the contents are really useful. And you can always offer to buy back clean copies at the end of the year.

You will of course need to approach the publishers of the original materials, explaining the circumstances in which they will be used (including any financial implications), and asking for permission to reproduce them. You will find that most publishers will be willing as long as you include an acknowledgement.

Use a textbook

There probably isn't one textbook on the market which contains exactly what you want your students to read. But there may be one which is close: if 75% of it is useful, you may have to decide that this is good enough, given the resource problems of the library, and require your students to buy it. You can tell them which parts you consider to be particularly good and perhaps concentrate more of your lecture and discussion time on the areas which in your view need elucidating or developing.

An advantage of many textbooks is that they include self-test questions as well as references and bibliographies. Using questions that other people have devised and tested is a good way of saving time and effort.

Complain

Get the support of your team and petition your head of department, faculty board, academic board, governors, etc. Urge your students also to complain through their union and representatives on committees and other bodies.

Students easily become socially isolated 9

Tutors don't usually take much interest in their students' social lives. Their relationship with them is a professional one which does not normally extend into social events apart from the occasional cup of coffee in the refectory. Students for their part have always organised their own social lives and relationships without asking their tutors for help.

Students can feel overwhelmed and intimidated by large numbers, however, and find informal social occasions difficult to organise. They can even have problems remembering the names and faces of their fellow students. The social isolation which more students are experiencing recently is not only distressing for them but also affects their work adversely: indeed, it is probably the factor which has most impact on their performance. It has become the responsibility of the tutors to try to help.

Induction socials
You can welcome students to your institution by organising a social during induction. This need not be an elaborate affair: what students appreciate is the opportunity to mix and talk to one another in an informal atmosphere. If numbers are very large, several socials can be held for separate groups, perhaps in major subject areas. If you enlist the help of established students and teaching assistants, or better still encourage them to take a lead in organising the social, this will make it more relaxed and enjoyable as well as making it easier to deal with the numbers.

Induction activities
Some induction programmes include group activities, simulations or games which serve as an introduction to the course and get students working together. An important by-product of these activities is that they foster social interaction.

Social interaction in seminars
Seminars in which students are given opportunities for interaction, by

learning one another's names, working together in sub-groups or teams and having brief social breaks, will not only foster learning but help students to feel less isolated.

Student parties
The best student parties are those which they organise themselves and, especially if you have given them a start during induction, you can expect them to take responsibility for their own social lives. You can, however, make a big difference by publicly supporting students who want to arrange a party. You can do this by giving them encouragement, helping them with practical details such as room bookings, and by turning up if they invite you.

Student photographs
Most courses have sheets of students' photographs displayed in the departmental office. You can be helpful to students if you pin up extra copies of their photographs in the corridor as well.

Students don't feel involved with the course 10

It is difficult for students to feel involved with their course when classes are large and contact with tutors is correspondingly distant. If their views are not sought or if they are not encouraged to engage with the material of the course, they easily become alienated and passive.

The best time to get students involved with the course is at the beginning. If they are in at the start, working with the issues of the course and influencing the way it runs, they will feel that the course belongs to them and the energy and motivation from this will carry them through. Some suggestions follow.

Initial group project
If you can start your course with a short group project which involves students in some action research in your discipline area, it is likely that during the task they will come up against many of the issues and problems which your course is designed to address and will produce their own mental map of the field. The small group work will also serve the additional purpose of encouraging students to get to know one another through working on a relevant and practical topic, and ease some of the social awkwardness which occurs at the beginning of a new group.

Chart of the course
Courses often begin with an overview lecture, which is followed up by meetings of discussion groups. To encourage your students to get the most out of the overview lecture you can ask each discussion group to produce a chart of the course, illustrating its structure, parameters, key elements, big issues etc. Students should be encouraged to supplement the material of the lecture with ideas from other sources and from their own discussion. The charts can be displayed in the lecture room in the second week.

Quiz
An unusual way to start a course is to set students a quiz in the first lecture session. The quiz should be designed in such a way that it provides an

overview of the course and obliges students to begin to apply themselves to some of the questions which the course deals with.

Pre-course meeting

A method of getting students involved, which is more radical because it requires them to negotiate the course content, is to organise a pre-course meeting, perhaps a couple of months prior to the start of the course. At this meeting each tutor presents a poster exhibition of his or her own area of expertise. Students are given an overview lecture and then view the exhibition. This is followed up by a library tour to help students to find relevant material. The students are then divided into seminar groups and given the task of devising the year's programme for their group and deciding which of them will be responsible for leading each seminar. While the students are doing this the tutors should be available in the exhibition area to answer queries and give advice.

If you use this model and are successful in getting students to take responsibility for the whole course in their seminars, you can dispense with lectures altogether. Alternatively students can devise a lecture programme, perhaps giving some of the lectures themselves, singly or in small groups.

Students don't get the individual help they need   **11**

Some students need a lot of individual help, others need less and some need little or none. In small classes, tutors get to know the students' individual needs and can respond to them flexibly. In large classes, there are more students who need help. They are also more difficult to identify. When numbers reach a certain size it is no longer possible for tutors to offer the same level of support to all students.

Funnelling

What is needed is a system of specifying broad categories of student need and funnelling the students so that those who need help at each stage can be identified and given the appropriate support. One way of doing this is described below. This system, if used effectively, is economical of staff time because it will ensure that most of the students will not use the expensive stages.

The system operates in four stages, but not necessarily in four consecutive teaching sessions.

a   Stage 1 is a weekly lecture which all students are required to attend.

b   Stage 2 is a follow-up testing and feedback session which all students, again, are required to attend. The tests can be of any kind as long as they are capable of being marked there and then by the students themselves so that they can get immediate feedback. Students who do well enough in the tests need not attend until the following week. Students who fail the tests continue to stage 3.

c   Stage 3 is a problem-solving session where the tutor responds to students' queries and helps them with their difficulties, perhaps taking them through some of the lecture material again and giving them examples to work on. Teaching assistants can also help in these sessions. Students who are now coping need not attend until the following week. Those who still have specific problems continue to Stage 4.

d   Stage 4 is a surgery held by the tutor for individual students. But there should be very few remaining who still need help.

Year tutor system

Another area in which students don't get the individual help they need is that of personal tutoring: with large numbers of students in their care personal tutors are now unable to carry out a role which was designed for small numbers.

Again, the answer is to look for ways of using the precious resource of staff time to offer help only to those students who really need it. This can be done by exchanging the personal tutor system, where staff have responsibility for monitoring the welfare of all their personal students, for a year tutor system. In this system, a few tutors are appointed to be responsible for each year of students. They advertise 'office hours' or 'surgery hours', where they are available to students who seek them out. So the responsibility shifts to the students to make contact with the tutors and ask for help only when they need it.

Students don't have independent learning skills

12

Conventionally, first year courses in higher education are taught cheaply, with large classes, a minimum of tutorials and very little personal contact or feedback. This is done so that more resources, in terms of staff time, can be invested in final year students, who tend to be very expensive to teach: dissertations are generally supervised individually and specialist options are taught in small classes.

This strategy has the drawback that the first year experience encourages students to be dependent: they become used to teacher-centred methods and are unable to take advantage of the opportunities for autonomy offered in the final year.

The way to avoid this is to invest more teacher time in the first year developing students' independent learning skills so that when they reach the final year they can cope with the demands of specialisation and exploit the opportunities for independent study. If they are able to take responsibility for themselves, access their own information and learn from one another, they will need less supervision and can be taught more cheaply.

For this to work, it is crucial to get it right in year one. A first year programme, aimed at developing students' independent learning skills, could include the following elements.

Study skills
Students need a grounding in study skills to be able to cope and feel confident about coping. For example, they need to be able to take useful notes, read effectively and efficiently, write well structured essays and reports, and cope with exams. If you want to teach them these skills yourself you can get some ideas from *53 Interesting ways of helping your students to study* in this series

of books.

Information skills
It is essential that students acquire the skills of accessing, extracting and processing information if they are to be able to study independently. And though with increasing numbers of students your library staff are no doubt less available for one-to-one assistance, they will probably be interested in working with you on programmes to help groups of students acquire such skills.

Problem-solving skills
Students need to develop problem-solving skills, initially to deal with the curriculum with which they are presently faced and subsequently in order to take their place in the workforce as competent practitioners in their chosen career.

You can help your students to develop these skills by devising some parts of your curriculum in terms of a series of problems of increasing complexity. Where students are unused to this way of working, you could start by posing problems where the task is clear and the solutions are achievable by the use of familiar procedures. The goal of this planned process will have been achieved when your students can tackle problems which are not well defined and whose solutions require them to use unfamiliar procedures.

One well known process of problem-solving typically involves 5 distinct stages:
a   identifying the problem
b   clarifying and refining it
c   generating solutions
d   choosing and implementing a preferred solution or solutions
e   monitoring and evaluating the chosen solution

Specific independent learning skills
Students need to be gently pushed into taking responsibility for themselves.

Instead of doing so much for them, you can help them to develop self direction and judgment by getting them to set themselves learning goals and practical tasks, monitor their own progress and correct their own work against given criteria. You can also encourage them to analyse how they organise their studying and how they arrive at decisions about the allocation of their time.

You can get further ideas from the PCFC booklet, *Independent learning with more students*[1].

Self-help groups

Students need practical and personal support. They can get this from one another if they form self-help groups, study groups, special interest groups or other kinds of student group. They will welcome your help in setting up their groups and also your advice on how to maintain a successful group. (For further suggestions see item 35.)

Feedback skills

If students are to learn to study independently of their tutors, they need to know how to give one another feedback. You can help them to clarify this by inviting them to draw up a set of guidelines. Give them a few minutes to note down examples of helpful and unhelpful feedback which they have received in the past from their teachers. Then ask them to pool suggestions for the guidelines, which you can put together on a handout for them.

[1] Gibbs, G. (1992) *Independent learning with more students*
ISBN 1 873576 15 8
(Available from OCSD, Oxford Brookes University, Oxford OX3 9AA)

Students don't feel valued 1.

It is difficult for students in large groups to feel that they matter. Often they don't know what's going on and they don't understand why restrictions are being placed on them. It seems to them that staff don't care what they think or even know who they are. They need to be shown in very deliberate ways that their involvement is valued and their opinions count.

Keep your students informed
Your students have the right to full information about institutional policies which affect them. They need to know why they are being taught in such large groups, why staff are frequently unavailable etc. They also need to know your view of the situation.

You could say, for example, 'The reason so many of you are packed into this lecture theatre is to do with the way the government is currently funding higher education. I've been told that this is the only way we can maintain a reasonable size for the discussion groups. I don't like it any more than you do. I haven't chosen to teach you in such large groups; it's been imposed on me'.

Or you could say, 'I can give you this much of my time and no more because this is how many students I have and I don't have any more hours in the week. I will do my best for you but I've come to the end of my resources'.

Ask your students to advise you
If you ask your students for advice, not only will you and they have the satisfaction of working together to make the best of a difficult situation but also you will receive plenty of useful suggestions from them: they are looking at things from a different angle and will come up with ideas which you haven't thought of.

You could say, for example, 'This is my problem. These are the numbers we've got. These are the course objectives. What advice would you give me?

What shall we do?' You can either ask students to note down their ideas and hand them in at the end of a lecture or you can invite student representatives to join you for a discussion of the group's responses.

Involve your students in decision making
Your students need to be informed about the decision making processes of your institution and encouraged to play their part to the full. Try to ensure that all your committees have student representatives. Impress upon them the importance of canvassing the views of their fellow students, attending meetings regularly, participating fully and generally making their contribution to the development of the course.

Learn your students' names
The better you know your students as individuals the more they will feel that they matter and their views are respected. The larger the student groups, the more necessary it is to make a real effort to learn students' names and remember who they are.

Staff feel powerless

The kind of rapid change which is being implemented in higher education, often without genuine consultation, makes staff feel distanced from their organisation, more apprehensive about their future, less trusting of all levels of management and generally powerless.

It is important that you look for areas, important to you, in which you can have some influence and ways in which your voice can be heard.

Get support for yourself
Identify colleagues who feel as you do about the situation in your institution. Discuss issues together and prepare yourselves in advance for meetings and other encounters so that you can support one another and not feel isolated.

You can also look to your union for support, particularly where they have negotiated conditions of service with the management.

Ask questions
Query decisions which affect you and your students. Ask for full explanations and clarifications until you are satisfied that you understand what is going on and why.

Stick to your principles
If you are clear about what is best educationally for your students and base your arguments on a sound educational rationale, this will act as a check on those of your colleagues who are interested only in questions of resources. You may in the end be able to achieve no more than a compromise with them but at least you will have ensured that the educational arguments have been heard.

Write to the papers
Write a letter to *The Higher*, the *Education Guardian*, to academic or professional journals, or other newspapers describing your situation, argu-

ɪg your case and proposing solutions. Send a copy of the letter to your union officers and to your management and stick a copy on your departmental notice-board.

Argue

Prepare arguments to support your case. Collect data so that you can back up your arguments with hard evidence. Find out, for example, how many photocopiers, computers, telephones and lavatories there are for student use and how many students there are for every seat in the library. Then tell your colleagues at your next section or department meeting.

Challenge

Look at the promotional material put out by your institution, and official documents such as mission statements and evaluation reports of the courses in your discipline area. Remind your institution and your colleagues of any claims to excellence, equal opportunities policies, commitment to access students or special provision of any kind and ask for resources necessary to fulfil these undertakings.

Look out for, and challenge, attempts made by management to deceive you. They might, for example, present fortnightly seminars as an innovative teaching method when in fact their motive is to save money or make staff redundant.

Resist

You do not have to accept a decision that is arbitrarily imposed upon you and your students. You can resist. Remember that there are formally established procedures in your institution for presenting a case all the way up the hierarchy. You can work through course committees, faculty boards, the academic board and board of governors; you can adduce the evidence of students, colleagues, external examiners, employers and H.M.I. And you can lobby other colleagues informally in order to obtain their support.

Some professional bodies, such as the Royal College of Nursing, the British Psychological Society and the Institute of Chartered Engineers, have a direct influence on the syllabuses of higher education courses and the academ standards which students are expected to meet. If in your institution tho. syllabuses are not being properly covered or the standards fully met, it is you, professional duty to bring this to the attention of the appropriate body, who will help you make a stand. Those of you who are external examiners on courses similar to yours in other institutions can be particularly effective in this regard.

Withdraw collaboration

You and your colleagues can resign publicly from committees, withdraw publicly from goodwill activities and generally refuse publicly to do more than is specified in your contract.

Chapter 2

Lectures

Informal lectures don't work any more

The informal lecture, with its impromptu explanations and humorous asides delivered in an intimate tone, is wasted on a large audience. Students at the back of the room are not able to assimilate - or perhaps even hear - what is being said.

As classes increase in size, so lectures need to be modified. They need to be structured more thoroughly, scripted more carefully and delivered more formally.

Structuring lectures

Your lecture may be structured according to questions and answers, problems and solutions, a chronological sequence, the development of an argument, a set of comparisons etc. It is important that you are aware of the structure and organise the lecture accordingly. It is also particularly important that you make the structure clear to your students by telling them what it is and reinforcing this with handouts, displays and reminders.

Scripting lectures

Most lecturers find that the only sure way to get across to a large audience is to structure the lecture clearly, write it down in full and read it out, word for word, or at least to have practised it sufficiently to have a script in their minds. (It is also an advantage to have a complete script if you intend to place a copy of your lecture in the library for students to consult.) And it will save you preparation time next year.

Delivery of lectures

You should deliver your lecture in a voice which is loud enough to be heard in all parts of the room and sufficiently varied in pitch to sound interesting. You will also need to speak more slowly if you are to enunciate your script clearly. And it is a good idea to rehearse your reading beforehand so that you can get the timing right.

If you have too many students for your lecture room, don't be tempted to fit them all in by seating them in the aisles or on the window sills. This presents not only an obstacle to learning but also a health and safety hazard. You have no option but to reduce the number of students in the room.

Videotape your lecture
A CCTV system will allow you to present your lecture on monitors in an overspill classroom. Such a system, once in place, requires little technician support or maintenance and can be operated by the lecturer. All you need to remember is to speak into the microphone and stand within the range and focus of the camera. For replay to the students a big-screen video replay system is an advantage.

At the same time as relaying the live lecture you can make a videotape copy of it which you can then use in a variety of ways. You can make it available, on reference only, in the library so that students can consult it and review sections they feel unsure of. Or you can arrange for a technician, a demonstrator or a student to put on a second showing of the lecture at another time in the week. These strategies are also helpful to students who missed the original lecture through absence or because of a timetable clash.

Watching a video recording of a lecture can be a poor substitute for a live performance so you should, if possible, provide lecture handouts to focus students' attention. You will also need to provide handouts of material which you are presenting on a screen or board in the lecture because this will not be clear on the video unless you have rostrum facilities. You can help students by explicitly referring to sections of these handouts during your lecture.

Give lectures to half the group at a time
Give your lecture twice. Get students to attend fortnightly, half the group at a time, and do directed reading between lectures.

...fuse to give the lecture
...end the students away and write a letter to your manager explaining why.

Resource-based learning

In the longer term, you can develop resource-based learning for your students. You can use ready-made materials which you purchase from the Open University or other institutions which have developed resource-based learning in your subject area. Or you can write your own materials, perhaps based initially on your lecture notes, though you will need to allow a substantial amount of time for preparing and piloting them. Your manager should be willing to allow you time to do this since the introduction of resource-based learning will result in substantial savings in your lecture time.

Get together with your colleagues

Compare notes with colleagues who teach the same students. Decide which is the best solution, educationally, for the students and present a joint case to your managers.

Students at the back can't read the overhead projector screen

As class sizes increase so students experience more difficulty in seeing material which is being presented to them at the front of the room. The board becomes redundant, demonstrations seem unintelligible and without great care even projected images are impossible to read.

If your overhead projection images cannot be seen from the back of the room you will need to make an adjustment in your methods of presenting material. Some suggestions follow.

Choice of equipment

Make sure you get the right overhead projector for the size of the room. In a large lecture theatre with seats for several hundred students you may find you need an image as big as 5 x 3 metres.

Brobdignagian writing

You can make the writing on the OHP transparency larger by using a broader OHP pen or by using a large typeface on a wordprocessor. (You will clearly need to spend time in the lecture room experimenting with different sizes of script but in a large room at least 18 point type will be required.) The implications of larger writing are of course that your diagrams will need to be simplified, your messages spread over several transparencies, and your production standards higher. You will need to use laser printed text rather than enlarged dot matrix text.

Handouts

Complicated diagrams or texts are often best presented on handouts. This method not only ensures that students will be able to see the material clearly but also that they will end up with a more accurate version of it.

Textbooks

There are of course resource problems which set a limit on how many

...douts can be given to large numbers of students. If your students have ...extbook which contains the material in question or similar material, your ...best plan is to refer them to the textbook, adapting your lecture if necessary to fit the book.

Students can't see the overall picture

Students who have a clear overall picture of the course and lecture programme find this helps them to understand, contextualise and integrate new material as it is presented to them. They also find it easier to relate it to their own reading and discussion activities.

Students can, however, easily lose sight of this structural framework and start seeing lectures as discrete packages of information. This happens particularly in large groups because of the formality of the occasion: with a large audience the lecturer is likely to pare down the lecture and avoid repetition, unscripted illustrations and informal explanations generally. Students in a large group also behave more formally and refrain from asking the lecturer to contextualise, connect or justify the material of the lectures, either in the lecture room or in the corridor afterwards.

Overview
You can be really helpful to your students if you give them an overview of the year's lecture course, either in linear form, or in the form of a diagram or chart. They will particularly appreciate it if you give them each a copy. To enable them to get the most out of it you can use it in one or more of the following ways.

- Draw students' attention to it at the beginning and end of the lecture course and from time to time during the course, to remind them what the whole of the programme is and what you have covered so far and to encourage them to anticipate what comes next.

- Use it as a focus for review particularly when you want to clarify and emphasise connections between parts of the course. You can also trace developments, pick out themes, identify gaps etc.

- Ask students to use it as a basis for making their own connections, groupings, emphases etc. Or ask students to draw diagrams of their own to illustrate these.

Students find it hard to concentrate

Students in lectures are able to pay attention for different lengths of time, but even a student with a good attention span will find it hard to concentrate for more than twenty minutes at a time. This has serious implications for students whose teachers use methods which are purely didactic.

The larger the size of the group the more difficult it is for students to concentrate on the lecture. They feel more remote from the lecturer and as a consequence the lecture has less immediacy for them, as well as being more difficult to hear. As members of a large group they find the experience impersonal. With large numbers of other students in the room there are lots of distractions. And the lecture room can easily become overheated and airless.

These problems need to be addressed by strategies which will, at intervals during the lecture, introduce different tasks and split down the group for short periods to enable the students to engage more actively with the lecture material. Some examples follow.

Review
Give students some time to review the lecture so far by looking through their notes or ask them to compare their lecture notes with their neighbour's.

Thinking time
Give students some time to think about the ideas which you have been presenting to them in the lecture.

Reading time
Give students some time to read a lecture handout or passage from the text book.

Copying time

Give students some time to copy down a diagram which you have presented to them and ask them some questions about it.

Unfinished sentences

Give students unfinished sentences which require an understanding of the lecture material for them to be completed.

Unfinished calculation

Ask students to complete a calculation or argument which you have begun.

Key points

Ask students to identify key points in the lecture.

Calculations

Set students one or two calculations which arise from the lecture material.

Application

Ask students to apply a concept described in the lecture to a given text, account, case, poem etc.

Discussion

Ask students to discuss a question or problem or issue in pairs.

All these activities can be done by students working individually or in pairs. (Groups of three or more are rather more difficult to organise, especially in a tiered lecture theatre.) To set up the activities you will need to make the following preparations.

• At the beginning of the lecture, forewarn students that you intend to introduce some activities for them to do. Give them a general idea of the kind of activity you have in mind and also a rationale for doing it: if students understand why they are being asked to do things they will get a lot more out of them.

- When you introduce an activity, make it absolutely clear what the students are supposed to be doing and how much time you intend to allow for it. It is helpful if you give them this in writing, maybe on a lecture handout or on the overhead projector. It is also necessary with large groups to warn students to watch or listen for the signal which you will use to bring the activity to a close: flashing the light on the OHP, clapping your hands, ringing a bell, raising your hand.

Students don't ask questions

Students need to be given the opportunity to ask questions in lectures so that they can check that their notes are accurate and that they have understood everything. Questions from students also help the lecturer to maintain contact with the class.

Even in small lecture groups, however, students are generally reluctant to ask questions: they are afraid that their fellow students will think that they are either arrogant or stupid. And in large lecture classes this becomes a major problem. Asking a group 'Are there any questions?' will generally elicit nothing but an embarrassed silence.

Make it easy for students to ask questions
The solution is to give students the chance to prepare their questions and discuss them with their neighbours before putting them to the lecturer. Students may also need reassurance about the acceptability of questions they want to ask; you could tell them, for example, that it's O.K. to check on dates and ask about the spelling of new names and difficult words as well as querying ideas and clarifying concepts.

As with anything else you intend to introduce into your lectures, you will need to forewarn students at the start. Tell them that you think it is very helpful for them - and you - if they ask questions so you are going to allow time for it. You could also suggest that they prepare themselves by writing a question mark in the margin of their notes whenever you say something that they are unsure about.

At the point in your lecture where you want them to formulate questions, you could say 'Now we come to question time. I'm going to give you three minutes to look through your notes and think of things that you'd like to ask questions about. There are bound to be some things that you'd like me to say again or explain or say more about - or maybe just *spell*. Please write down your questions'.

After three minutes, say to the class 'Now I' d like you to get into pairs and see if you can answer each other's questions. Maybe you'll find your partner answers some of your questions very adequately and so you won't want to bring forward those questions. Make a note of any outstanding questions that you and your partner would like to put to me. I'll take any questions in three minutes' time'.

After three minutes, say 'O.K., now we've got some time for questions. Who'd like to start?'

In large classes it can be very difficult to tell if students are learning anything from the lecture. Their faces are often too far away for you to read their expressions. They are unlikely to ask or answer questions in public. In fact, there is often no communication at all from the audience to the lecturer. And for the students themselves, sitting in large lecture classes can be such a passive experience that they too are unsure what they are learning.

The following methods enable you and your students to check how much they are learning in your lectures.

Quiz
A short quiz of perhaps three questions can be administered. First, students need to be forewarned that you intend to ask them some questions at the end of the lecture. You should explain to them that this is not so much a test as an opportunity for them - and you - to check that they have understood and assimilated the lecture. You could also reassure them that you will not pounce on anyone.

You can process students' answers to the questions in one of a number of ways.

• Collect up the anonymous answers, just to find out what your students have understood. You can then give a short remedial overview at the start of your next lecture.

• Give instant answers so that students can check for themselves how much they have understood.

• Use a show of hands (see also below) after you have provided answers, to see how many students have got them right.

- Get students to pair up with their neighbours and mark or comment on each other's answers.

Show of hands
Students may be prepared to respond to a request for a show of hands in answer to questions of the following types.

'Here is the answer to the calculation I just gave you. Who managed to get it right?'

'How many of you would like me to go back over this with more examples before I go on to the next topic?'

'So to see if I've explained clearly enough the ways of analysing the data, who thinks you should use the X method? ... the Y method? ... the Z method?'

Shows of hands can be used easily and quickly once students trust that you are using them to guide your teaching, rather than to make judgments about individuals.

Instant questionnaire
You can give students an instant questionnaire to assess how much they are learning. Display a set of statements of the following type and ask students to rate each one on the scale: 5 = strongly agree; 1 = strongly disagree.
I feel confident about .....
I could explain .....
I need to spend more time on .....
I could use the X method .....
I feel confused about .....

You can collect up and collate students' responses and use them to modify your next lecture.

Students' notes

It can be very revealing to photocopy or borrow several students' notes (different students each week) and look through them to see what the students consider to be important, what they appear to misunderstand, and what they take down verbatim without seeming to think about it.

It is helpful to students if you inform them of any conclusions you come to as a consequence of looking at their notes or collating their questionnaire responses.

The lecture isn't enough

The larger the number of students the more difficult it is for the lecturer to gauge the appropriate level and pace for the lecture. Students may therefore need parts of the lecture to be repeated or clarified but in large groups they feel inhibited about requesting this either during the lecture or later: teachers with large numbers of students are known to be too busy to have time for individuals.

One way of addressing this problem, which gives all students the opportunity to get the most out of the lecture, is to provide them with supporting material. This material can take various forms.

Scripts or recordings
If you read your lectures verbatim you may want to make copies of the script available to your students. Alternatively, you may prefer to make audiotapes of your lectures. There is a range of simple recording devices currently available, comprising a small tape recorder and a lapel microphone, which give quite satisfactory recordings for this purpose. Scripts or audiotapes can be placed in the library for students to borrow.

Notes
If you give your lectures from notes you may want to give your students copies of your notes together with a summary of the lecture, references, and paper copies of any OHP transparencies. Or you can make a few copies of these available in the library. This is also very helpful for any colleagues who run discussion groups which are based on your lectures as well as for students with disabilities that prevent them from taking lecture notes easily.

Textbooks
If you base a series of lectures on a single textbook you can be helpful to your students if you inform them of this so that they can use the textbook to contextualise and improve their notes. Further, if the lecture course is

very closely related to the textbook, you may want to give your students the option of attending the lectures or working from the textbook instead, either individually or in self-help groups. A summary of the lecture programme, together with references to sections of the book, will enable them to do this quite easily. Lecturers who have offered students this choice have found that there was no difference in exam performance between those students who attended the lectures and those who worked alone or in groups. And if enough of your students opt to miss some or all of your lectures this may incidentally help to reduce your accommodation problems.

Study guides

In the long term, it may be possible for you to produce study guides to accompany your lecture courses. The study guide is a device to enable students to work with lecture material, set texts or material from other sources in the absence of the teacher. It consists of a set of preparatory activities, follow-up activities and self-assessment exercises based on the course material which enable the students to get the most out of the course by answering questions, asking themselves questions, solving problems, doing calculations etc.

If you want to write a study guide for your students, you can get detailed instructions from David Kember's *Writing study guides*, Technical & Educational Services, 1992.

There isn't time to cover the syllabus 23

In many institutions, staff contact with students is being cut back as a response to increased numbers. Because they have less contact overall with students, staff are trying to cover more and more material in their lectures. Add to this the extra time it takes to lecture to a large group and the rate at which all subject areas are developing, and it is not surprising that many lecturers are anxious about the possibility of covering the syllabus.

If you feel pressure on the lecture time which students have with you, you may like to try some or all of the following changes.

Change the syllabus
If you are working with a syllabus which you devised yourself, you can change it so that it contains less material.

Change the lecture
If you are unable to change the syllabus because you are preparing your students for assessment by some professional or other external body, you can make better use of your time if you change the way you use the lecture.

You can no longer expect to tell the students everything you want them to know: you will need to think carefully about your aims and prioritise material so that the lecture time is spent in the most productive way. So, for example, if you gave students a lecture on a chapter in their textbook you would be making less efficient use of the time than if you offered them additional examples to those in the chapter or a critical comparison of materials drawn from a variety of sources.

Change the role of the students
If the lecture content is cut back, students will need to take responsibility for covering some of the syllabus themselves, either on their own or in study groups. For this to be successful you will need to be absolutely clear

in your instructions and explanations when you set them work to do. You will also need to ensure that they learn how to access information, how to read effectively and how to be critical of what they read.

Complain

Write a report on your situation and present it to management through the official channels. Send a copy to your professional association and also to any external body or examiner who needs the information.

Students find big lectures uninspiring   24

As more resources are put into large groups with the corresponding deterioration in informal personal contact between staff and students, lectures are going to have to do more than just impart information. Students' motivation, involvement and commitment will depend very heavily on what happens in lectures. One way of encouraging this is to develop student participation (as explained in items 19, 20 and 21). Or you can deliver inspirational lectures.

Inspirational lectures
When preparing an inspirational lecture, remember that its inspirational function may be its most important feature. Spend time thinking of what will excite and enthuse your students rather than concentrating solely on getting the content right. Try to make it a happening which they will remember. Here are some ideas you may wish to try.

• Try to make your lecture presentation challenging and exciting. Think of ways of projecting your voice and your enthusiasm. Don't be afraid, in front of a large audience, to speak in a strong, authoritative voice and amplify your gestures.

• Borrow ideas from the entertainment industry. Go for noise, colour, action. Experiment with visual displays, background music, dramatic interludes and staged interruptions.

• Use extracts of video or film, not just for students to watch but as an integral part of the lecture, so that part of the job of inspiring students is done by the visual media.

• Invite a colleague to share a lecture with you in which the two of you debate alternative ways of tackling a problem or present alternative viewpoints on the same topic, perhaps even role playing the proponents of two opposing views.

- 'Star' performers in many disciplines regularly visit learned societies and higher education institutions in major cities. You can help your students by informing them of such flying visits and encouraging some of them to attend. You may wish to set aside some time in which those who manage to attend can report back on the experience to their peers.

Chapter 3

Discussion groups and seminars

25 Students feel anonymous in large discussion groups
26 There are too many students to sit in a circle
27 Students find it hard to prepare for discussion groups
28 Large discussion groups easily lose direction
29 There's too much inconsistency between parallel groups
30 Groups are too big for all the students to participate
31 Some groups are just too big for any kind of seminar
32 Tutors feel unsure of their new role
33 There are too many students to teach them all every week
34 Students can't be expected to give seminar papers in large groups
35 Students lack groupwork skills
36 There aren't enough classrooms for student groups

Students feel anonymous in large discussion groups   **25**

In a large group students find it difficult to make contributions to the discussion by asking questions or sharing ideas if they feel that they hardly know one another.

And yet the name games and other introductory activities which work so well in small groups would be unwieldy with large numbers. What is needed is a simple, effective method of ensuring that students at least know the name of everybody in their group. Two such methods are described here. (If these methods are to work, you will need to convince students that making the effort to learn names, though potentially embarrassing, is actually very valuable and you will need to insist that they take it seriously. It will help if you join in.)

Name labels
The most popular method of identifying people, in education generally and particularly at conferences, is to use labels, either a gummed address-type label which people stick to their clothes or a piece of folded card which they can prop up on the table in front of them.

Sometimes this method does not work very well, either because people write their names using a pen with too fine a line or because they forget to bring their labels to the second and subsequent meetings of the group. At the risk of seeming tiresome you will need to specify that students write their names clearly, with a broad pen. And you will need to bring extra labels to each meeting of the group until all members know one another's names.

Lists
Meetings and other group activities often begin with all members saying their names in turn round the group. This serves as a general introduction but in no way ensures that people then know one another's names. For this

to be achieved people will have to exercise their memories in a series of name repetitions.

a   Ask group members to say their names in turn and ask everyone as this is happening to write down all the names in a list.

b   Suggest that everyone writes notes, or draws a picture or other memory aid, next to each name to help them remember which name belongs to which person.

c   Give them some time to learn the names. Warn them that you are going to test them.

d   Ask them to turn their notes face down and see if they can remember the names of the rest of the group. They could do this with their neighbour if they wanted.

e   Ask volunteers to repeat the names round the group. Urge those who do not volunteer to have a go.

f   Get the whole group to change places, and try again.

g   Ask volunteers to raise their hands at random. As an individual raises his or her hand, the other group members call out the person's name.

h   Finally, suggest that for homework all group members revise the names, using their notes, so that they still know them at the next meeting.

You can reinforce this exercise by organising students immediately afterwards in a work-related activity which requires that they interact with one another, perhaps in teams, and ensures that they appreciate the value of knowing one another.

It is also very helpful to students if you always use their names when you speak to them and encourage them to do the same.

There are too many students to sit in a circle   **26**

For generations students in discussion groups have sat in a circle: the obvious arrangement if they are to communicate with one another verbally and non-verbally.

Student sub-groups

The tutor who is faced with a group which is too large to sit in a circle is not, however, obliged to seat the students in rows and lecture to them. The simple alternative is to arrange them in groups of three, four, five or six depending on the task that they are to engage in. Discussions and other activities then take place in these sub-groups rather than in the group as a whole.

The easiest way to organise these separate groups is to set up the chairs in the classroom before the students arrive so that as they come in and sit down they find themselves in groups of the appropriate size. Or you can draw a diagram on the board with an instruction to students to set up the chairs accordingly. You will obviously have more space if you are able to stack up any tables and put them in a corner before you start. (For suggestions about mixing the groups, see item 31.)

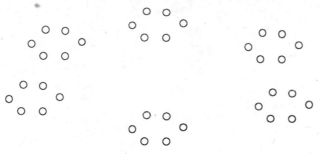

This arrangement may also have the advantage of making each sub-group more accessible if you want to move around between them (see item 32).

Students find it hard to prepare for discussion groups   27

Students put more into a discussion and get much more out of it if they do some relevant preparation beforehand. Good preparation is even more important in a situation where resources are diminishing and students have fewer tutor-led sessions and less personal contact with staff: they need to optimise the use of their time with the tutor.

Course booklet
If the groups are large, however, students tend to find preparation difficult. This is because they do not feel the kind of membership of the group and commitment to it which are characteristic of smaller and more intimate groups. They also have more problems getting hold of set reading from the library. When a course has a large number of parallel groups, access to the set reading materials can become impossible. Students in this situation need the help of a specially written booklet.

Your booklet can include some or all of the following.
*   A conceptual overview of the course, giving outlines of the discussion topics, reasons why they have been chosen and explanations of how they fit into the course.

*   Objectives for each session with lists of learning outcomes to be aimed for.

*   Discussion questions for each session.

*   Advice on how to prepare for each session, including library information and hints on reading and note-taking.

*   A description of the characteristics of a successful session, together with advice on how to avoid being difficult and how to deal with others

who are being difficult. This can include checklists to help students to review the way they run their own sessions (see item 35).

- Advice on how to (and how not to) give seminar presentations, together with an offer of brief tutorial support before such presentations.

- Annotated reading lists for each session, providing guidance on the strengths and weaknesses of the books and pointing out their theoretical stance, usefulness for particular issues, and so on.

- Alternative reading lists, suggesting a wider range of sources.

- Copies of key readings, arguments, diagrams etc.

- Explanations of any special teaching methods used.

- Explanations of mechanisms and criteria for tutor assessment and peer assessment.

- Exhortations to take the sessions seriously, backed up, if possible, by positive feedback from last year's students.

Large discussion groups easily lose direction 28

The larger the group the easier it is for discussion to become fragmented, contradictory and unwieldy. There are too many conflicting interests and perspectives in a large group for it to run in a constructive way without the introduction of something to give shape to the proceedings.

Agenda
You can give your teaching sessions shape and direction by drawing up an agenda for each one. This will ensure that students know what is supposed to be happening and what topics the group is supposed to be addressing. It will also make it much easier for them to keep themselves and one another on track and to the point.

An agenda can take the form of a list of topics to be covered or questions to be answered or problems to be tackled or readings to be discussed, or a mixture of these. It is helpful if the items on the list are self-explanatory phrases rather than single words.

You can treat the agenda formally by setting out the items on a printed sheet and handing out copies to the students either at the beginning of the session or, preferably, at the end of the preceding meeting of the group. Or you can adopt a more collaborative approach and ask students to propose agenda items which you then list on the board. You can also ask them to rate the items in terms of importance and make proposals as to how much time the group should spend on each.

Once students are used to working to an agenda they can carry forward this practice into their student groups.

There's too much inconsistency between parallel groups   29

A familiar way of organising teaching in higher education is for the weekly lectures to a whole class to be followed up by parallel seminar or discussion groups in which the lecture material can be clarified, discussed and developed. A class of forty students might be split into four seminar groups of ten all taught by the same tutor. But now that institutions are taking on many more students, we are seeing classes of five hundred split into twenty-five parallel seminar groups of twenty. It takes a large team of tutors to handle such multiple groups and this brings with it a wide range of problems.

With such a large number of groups there is likely to be great variation in the work of different groups: what topics are discussed, what processes are used, and what outcomes are achieved. It is difficult to maintain an overview of the work so that students in different groups have a comparable experience and are equally fitted to cope with the assessment. (This is particularly important if assessment is by means of a final examination.) This difficulty is compounded if the team includes tutors who are not otherwise involved in the teaching of the course or part-time teachers who are not available for extra meetings.

To achieve consistency and equity in parallel groups, the course leader will need to establish a range of procedures of the following type. (Decisions should be made as far as possible in consultation with the members of the staff team; where members of the team such as part-time teachers are not able to participate they must be kept fully informed by letter.)

Notes for tutors
Before the course begins, draw up a set of notes for tutors, specifying the course objectives and programme. Give a copy to all members of the staff team. If you have written a booklet for students (see item 27), enclose a copy. Include also full information about deadlines, regulations and

criteria for assessment.

Lecture summaries
Arrange for staff giving the lectures to provide a summary of each lecture, together with copies of any handouts used. Distribute these to all members of the team.

Hints for tutors
Offer hints for running groups (see items 26, 28 and 30).

Handouts
Put together a file of handouts for the course and invite members of the team to use material from it.

Events
Remind tutors about events in other parts of the course, e.g. visiting speakers or field trips.

Assessment questions
Ask all members of the team to contribute questions for coursework assessment and examinations. (Do this well in advance.) Call meetings to agree the essay title lists and examination question papers. Distribute copies of these to all team members.

Meetings
Call regular meetings of the team to maintain an overview and deal with difficulties and queries. Make a note of decisions made at these meetings and distribute copies of your notes to all team members.

Groups are too big for all the students to participate   **30**

In a small discussion group it is possible for a skilled tutor to facilitate communication between students so that they feel at ease with one another and can confidently participate in a free-ranging discussion. They can engage in exploratory talk, which is how students in a successful discussion group try out their ideas and deepen their understanding. But as soon as the group size increases beyond eight or ten students, the relaxed atmosphere and the sense of space are lost and many students become reluctant to join in. And in very large discussion groups there is not enough time for all students to use exploratory talk even if they wanted to.

The answer is to structure the work of the group so that students are operating, for some of the time at least, in smaller units. Some suggestions follow.

Sub-groups
If students work in sub-groups for part of the session this will ensure that they all have the chance to speak and explore ideas with others. A method that works well is to begin by presenting students with some introductory information and challenging material and then to get them to work in sub-groups on specific questions or discussion topics for the main part of the session. (Remember to make it clear to them before they start precisely what the task is and how much time you have allowed for it.)

You can bring the whole group together at the end for ten minutes of plenary discussion or questions or, if the situation merits it, you can invite a spokesperson from each sub-group to summarise the group's conclusions.

(For suggestions about the arrangement of furniture, see item 26. For suggestions about the role of the tutor while students are working in sub-groups see item 32.)

Thinking time

In a large discussion group there is not enough time for all students to speak at any length. (Twenty students in a one-hour session have an allowance of only three minutes each, - even if the tutor says nothing at all.) But all the students are having individual thoughts and interesting ideas. So that these do not get lost, you can intersperse other activities with periods set aside for quiet reflection and individual note-taking. The ideas or notes which are produced can either be deemed to be for the students' personal benefit or they can be carried forward into work in the sub-groups. An incidental advantage of doing this is that students learn that silences in discussion groups are not necessarily 'embarrassing' or 'painful' but can be a condition for creative thinking.

Consequences

This activity brings together aspects of those described in the two preceding sections. Students first have some thinking time in which to write a statement, a question or some notes, depending on the objectives of the session. They then pass their pieces of paper round their sub-group in the manner of the game of *Consequences*, writing additions onto each paper as it comes round. By reading other people's ideas students are stimulated into making interesting and varied responses. They are also engaging in an activity - writing - which is likely to be more closely related to their course assessment than oral discussion.

Fishbowl

If from time to time you want to change the disposition of the group members quite radically, you can organise a fishbowl discussion. In a fishbowl, participants sit in two concentric circles and adopt different roles: those in the inner circle engage in discussion, while those in the outer circle remain silent and observe the others. After a given length of time - say ten minutes - those on the outside give feedback to those on the inside or the two groups change places and roles.

This method was developed for use in interpersonal skills training so that the observers can give feedback to the members of the inner circle about their behaviour in a group. You can use it for this purpose or you can introduce it in a situation when you want to highlight difference: members of the two circles can act as representatives of opposing theoretical arguments or value positions or practical approaches. Or, if you are happy to cope with students' strong feelings, you can separate women and men or school leavers and mature students etc.

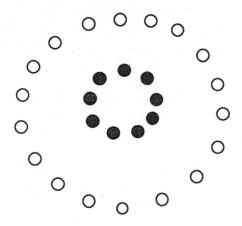

Some groups are just too big for any kind of seminar 31

Some classes these days are clearly far too large for any useful learning to take place without fundamental reorganisation of the group. One way of doing this is to divide up the group and teach sub-groups in rotation (see item 33). Another way is to introduce workshops into your programme. (Or you could of course do both.)

A workshop involves a sequence of structured tasks and discussions which are designed to enable participants to tackle problems, address issues and to develop their thinking on a given topic.

By working in groups of varying sizes and moving from group to group, participants have the opportunity to exchange ideas with a variety of other people. Three workshop activities which enable this kind of mobility are described here. The purpose of the first one, *moving clockwise*, is simply to mix the groups; the purpose of the second one, *envoys* or *crossovers*, is to disseminate discussion points as they are carried forward from one group to another; the purpose of the third one, *pyramid*, is to challenge and develop the views of individuals. You will want to select the activity which serves your purpose best in terms of the objectives of the workshop.

Moving clockwise
a   Students do an exercise in groups of 3. (This activity is easier to organise if the groups of 3 are arranged in a circle around the room.)
b   Ask the students in each group to take a letter A, B or C. Then tell them that, in order to mix the groups, the A's should stay put, the B's should join the next group and the C's should join the next group but one, moving clockwise round the room. They are then ready to do a second exercise in newly constituted groups.
c   If you want students to do a third or subsequent exercise in new groups, just repeat the instructions.

Envoys/Crossovers

a   Ask students to form groups. The number of groups can be determined by the number of different themes which you identify but there should be as near as possible the same number of students in each group.

b   Describe the activity to the students and explain that each person will be expected to carry forward the ideas of their group into other, new groups.

c   Allocate an aspect of the workshop topic to each group of students. Give the students some time to discuss their themes.

d   Ask the students in each group to take the letter A, B, C, D etc. Then get them to form new groups in which all the A's are together, all the B's are together etc. These new groups, which will contain representatives who have been primed to speak on all the aspects of the topic, will be in a good position to tackle the topic as a whole.

Pyramid

a   Give students a short task to do individually, e.g. you could ask them to answer a question, write notes on a topic, criticise material presented on a handout etc.

b   Get students to form pairs and give them some time to discuss the task and compare notes.

c   Get the pairs to join together to make groups of four. Ask these groups to identify general principles, criteria, theories etc. which arise from the individual and pairs work.

It is crucial in running any of these activities that you give students a rationale for your choice of method as well as precise instructions about what they are supposed to do at each stage and a clear statement of how much time they have in which to do it. They will also need to be reminded to check out the names of the other people they are working with at each stage.

Tutors feel unsure of their new role   32

There are some teaching situations in which large numbers of students may be divided up into smaller groups. This can happen where the tutor decides to split the class into sub-groups for discussion (see item 30) or where one tutor has overall responsibility for a set of parallel groups. In either case the tutor's job is to tour round the groups, spending a short time with each one.

Touring
In this situation, the traditional role of the tutor is no longer appropriate; a new role is needed which is supportive of students and allows the tutor an overview of their progress but without inhibiting their discussion.

You can be helpful to your students if you remember these principles when visiting the groups.
- Join the groups quietly and unobtrusively. Make it clear that you don't intend to take over the discussion.
- Let things run for a while. Don't intervene until you have understood what is going on and then only if you are sure that the students really need your help.
- Stay quiet if you possibly can.
- Leave if you feel things are going well, even if you haven't said anything since you arrived. Don't be tempted to stay until you have eventually intervened, just to prove that you were needed.
- You don't have to spend the whole session rushing from one group to another. This might lower your anxiety but it would not be helpful to the groups. After a few sessions you could try visiting some of the groups and not others.

When you do need to contribute to the work of a group, try to adopt one of the following roles.

Process consultant

The students may not be very good at handling the process of their group, even if they are managing the content successfully. The tutor can point out what appears to be going well or badly ('You seem to be getting through the agenda really well, but I wonder if you are moving on a bit too quickly') and suggest alternative ways to work ('It seems as though only three of you are involved in the discussion. Perhaps if you found out what everyone thinks at each stage you might have more to discuss').

Subject expert

Groups may want you to provide missing information, clarify a point or act as arbiter in a dispute. These can be difficult interventions to judge because you don't want the groups to become dependent on you. Look for ways of encouraging them to deal with things themselves. And don't give them a mini-lecture in answer to a simple factual question.

Facilitator of independent learning

Groups may need help in recognising what is going on in the group. You could ask them 'What's happening in this group at the moment?' and if they give a reply like 'Well, we seem sort of bogged down' you could ask, 'How are you bogged down?' or 'How did this come about?'

They may also need help in taking their own steps to do something about the problems. You could ask them 'What might get you out of the bog?' then 'Which of you is going to do that?' and 'How can you avoid falling into a bog again?'

The overall aim should always be to develop a group's ability to manage without you, rather than to make yourself indispensable through your brilliant interventions.

There are too many students to teach them all every week 33

Educationalists have always argued that it is fruitful for students to spend time learning from one another without a tutor: students speak the same language, they see problems from a similar perspective and they feel happier about asking questions of fellow students. Student groups are not only to be recommended for educational reasons; with diminishing resources they have become a necessary part of the programme in situations where staff want to be able to continue to work with groups of a reasonable size.

Alternate student groups with tutor-led groups
Patterns of alternating student groups with tutor-led groups vary: if, as in the diagram below, you have a group of 24 students which is scheduled to meet weekly, you can split them into two groups of 12 and teach each group fortnightly or you can intersperse workshops for the whole group of 24 among the meetings of smaller groups. In timetabled slots where the tutor is teaching another group, students can work very usefully together.

Tutor-led sessions and student-only sessions lend themselves to different types of activity. Use tutor-led sessions to impart information, give students feedback on their progress, deal with their problems, answer their questions etc. and to brief them for their next student-only session. Activities which are best left to the student groups include preparation for and discussion of tutor-led sessions, and subsequent recapitulation, consolidation and integration which could include group assignments, checktests, problem-solving, case studies, calculations etc. Students working without a tutor can also take responsibility for running their own seminars (see item 34).

It is very important when setting up a programme of this kind to be sure that students understand why they are meeting in student groups. And it is essential to ensure that they have a varied programme of relevant and

97

challenging activities if they are to obtain full benefit from working together.

Group A (12 students) meets with tutor	Group B (12 students) meets with tutor	Workshop Tutor with all 24 students	Independent student work or work in independent sub-groups
Week 1 →	Week 2 →	Week 3 →	Week 4 →
← Week 5 →	Week 6 →	Week 7 →	Week 8 →
← Week 9 →	Week 10 →	Week 11 →	Week 12 →

For ways of helping students to develop their groupwork skills, see item 35.

Tell the truth
Students have the right to know beforehand that they are going to be taught for only half the timetabled time. If you plan to operate this scheme, you must warn them of it in the prospectus and remind them of it in the student handbook.

Students can't be expected to give seminar papers in large groups   34

When asked to identify ways in which their course helps them to acquire personal transferable skills, many students select the reading of a seminar paper to a group as one of those activities which most help them to gain confidence. If as part of the exercise they are also expected to encourage and chair the subsequent group discussion, they find the experience even more helpful.

There are of course several potential problems for students associated with this method of learning. The student who is giving the paper generally finds the experience intimidating. The tutor often finds it difficult to resist interrupting the student or even taking over completely. The other members of the group can find themselves adopting a passive role and so stop preparing for seminars except when it is their turn to give the paper.

These problems, which have always been potential hazards, are much more likely to be encountered in large seminar groups.

Student-only seminars
This method of working offers an excellent opportunity for students to work in a group without a tutor. If there is no tutor present, many of the problems associated with power and authority are removed. In addition, you can make the groups as small as you like, especially early on in the course, so that the student reading the paper is not so intimidated and the other students have more opportunity to participate actively. And the smaller you make the group the more opportunities to lead the group each student will have.

Unless they are used to working unaided, students engaging in this venture will need your help in setting it up. They will probably appreciate it if you do some or all of the following.

- Negotiate a programme of topics with the students. (It is likely, however, that they will prefer to arrange informally among themselves the question of who tackles which topic.)

- Suggest that in the first instance they give the seminar papers in pairs or at least that the student giving the paper prepares it in discussion with a fellow student.

- Give them the usual help with references to reading which will be useful in preparing for the seminars.

- Make it clear where and how they can contact you if they want more references or help of any other sort.

- Encourage them not only to prepare their seminar papers but also to write out lists of questions on their topic which they can put to the group to facilitate discussion.

- If you are concerned that students may not take such presentations seriously with no tutor present, you can introduce peer assessment (see items 51 and 52).

For more details on helping students to work without a tutor, see item 35.

Students lack groupwork skills   35

Several items in this chapter (e.g. items 33, 34 and 47) entail students working in groups without a tutor. This is to be recommended, not only because it helps solve the problem of large classes but also because it fosters in students the skills of collaboration, team work and social interaction.

While group work develops skills, however, it also requires skills. If you leave a group of students alone without preparing them for group work, it is likely that all they will learn is that group work is very difficult and uncomfortable. Learning to work together, share tasks, devise and keep to schedules, support one another and trust one another does not come quickly or without effort. If your students have never worked in groups without a tutor, you will need to help them develop their skills and take time to look at what goes wrong and what can be done to make things go right. They will also need help in planning discussion sessions and reassurance from you that they are capable of working on their own. Some suggestions follow.

Names
It is crucial that members of the group know one another's names if they are to be able to communicate well. Make sure that your students know everyone's name before you leave them alone. (For suggestions on how to achieve this, see item 25.)

Ground rules
If a group has ground rules, its members have a clearer idea of what is expected of them and what is permitted. Help your students to draw up ground rules for themselves and ask them to decide what they are going to do if anyone breaks a rule. You can also encourage them to amend or add to the rules as the work of the group develops.

Confidentiality
If members of the group are to trust one another, they will need to agree on confidentiality. The form of words should be discussed but it could be, for example, 'We agree not to repeat outside the group anything of a personal nature that anyone says in the group'.

Difficult situations
Work with the group on tasks which highlight issues and problems of group interaction such as decision making, team work, self disclosure, competition.

Difficult students
Get the group to discuss strategies for coping with students who are habitually absent, silent, dominating, negative etc.

Observers
Use a couple of members of the group as observers and ask them to report on what they notice.

Tape recording
Record a session with the group and ask them to listen to the tape and say what they hear.

Fishbowl (see item 30)
Ask the students in the outer circle to look specifically at the group dynamics of the inner circle.

Questions
Give students a task to do in sub-groups. Then ask them to reflect on the dynamics of their group by asking them questions such as:
    'What methods did you use to come to decisions in your group?'
    'Who was the leader?'
    'Did some people speak more than others or was it about equal?'

Roles

Ask all students to write a short piece entitled 'My role in this group'. Put all the papers in a hat and redistribute them. Students then read out the description they have drawn from the hat and the group tries to guess who wrote it.

Monitoring group processes

Ask everyone to write down answers to the four questions:

'What's going wrong in this group?'
'What's going right?'
'What could I do about it?'
'What could other people do about it?'

Then ask them to discuss what they have written.

Agenda (see item 28)

Get students into the habit of setting agendas for sessions with you so that they can continue to do so when they start to work alone.

Rotating chair

Get students to take turns leading the discussion. You can lend them a copy of *53 Interesting things to do in your seminars and tutorials* to give them ideas.

Reminder

Remind students of the activities you have done with them and encourage them to use them again as needed, to help them with their group processes.

Tips

Lodge half a dozen copies of *53 Interesting things to do in your seminars and tutorials* in the department office or on the library issue desk for students to consult before running a discussion session.

Safety net

Tell the students that, though you are going to leave them, you are not going to abandon them. Tell them when and where they can contact you if they need to, either as a group or as individuals.

There aren't enough classrooms for student groups   36

With increasing numbers of students in higher education, classroom space generally is under pressure. If this is a problem for staff teaching on regular courses, it is even more of a problem for those who need extra space so that their students can operate in workshop sub-groups, project groups or other student groups.

If your students have difficulty finding a place to meet, you could make some or all of the following suggestions to them.

Meet at unpopular times
They could meet early in the morning or at the end of the day or in the lunch break or on Wednesday or Friday afternoons. Those who live in the area could meet during holidays: this has the advantage of offering them continuity of contact with their fellow students.

Meet in available places
There may be rooms in your institution which, while not being designed as classrooms, make acceptable meeting places for student groups. There is often space in the refectory outside meal times, for example, and indeed many students find it easier to work together in an informal setting of this kind.

Make official bookings
You, or your students, could speak with the person responsible and book classrooms officially. This would have the added advantage of bringing this aspect of the accommodation problem to the notice of the administrators and management.

Make their own arrangements
If all else fails, student groups will have to find their own accommodation, either in other public places or in their own homes.

Complain
Encourage students to report on the lack of accommodation through the usual course evaluation channels.

Chapter 4

Practicals, projects and fieldwork

There isn't room in the laboratory for all the students   37

Laboratories are generally designed in such a way that the space is fixed and the number of student places is limited. This means that, if the number of students on your course doubles, you have the choice of running twice as many laboratory sessions or teaching the students half as often, unless you can find other accommodation in which to work. Two alternative types of accommodation are classrooms and lecture rooms. You can use these two very effectively in combination with laboratories if you take care to identify the best use of each one for your needs.

Laboratories
If your students are to spend only half the statutory time in the laboratory, you will need to give careful thought to which of the experiments or investigations you wish to retain. This will involve you in reviewing your objectives for practicals and separating out those sessions which students need to experience from those which they can just as usefully observe.

Classrooms
An ordinary classroom can be used for those parts of the experimental work which do not require a laboratory: working with data and writing up practicals. You could take the opportunity here to run workshops to help students to develop the skills of data interpretation and scientific communication.

Lecture rooms
There are many procedures which students do not need to be able to perform themselves in a laboratory but which they need to have seen demonstrated in order to have a visual idea of the process and a sense of the scale and complexity of the equipment etc. These can be demonstrated in a lecture room. The demonstrations can be performed live by a member of staff or, if you have very large groups of students, you may prefer to

work with video or computer images which can be projected onto a large screen.

Computer programmes have also been developed to enable students to do simulated experiments. You can display data on the screen, get students to experiment by inputting variables or selecting different courses of action from the menu presented and the computer will process and display the results.

Briefing students for practicals is too time-consuming 38

Supervising laboratory work for large numbers of students, especially when practicals are duplicated to accommodate extra students, can involve lecturers and demonstrators in very repetitive briefings and explanations. These take up a great deal of staff time and also waste precious time in the laboratory. Much of the material which might otherwise be presented in briefings at the start of practicals can however be prepared on paper in advance and given to students in the form of a lab guide.

Lab guides
There are some kinds of laboratory work where lab guides are invaluable: where practicals are predetermined, students use standard techniques and outcomes are predictable. In order to justify production costs for the guide you also need, as well as a large number of students, practicals which are a required part of the students' programme and will remain unchanged for some years. Some colleges operate successful systems of standardised laboratory work based on lab guides, though even these do not remove all need for briefing: the only foolproof briefing is one which is written, and followed, like a computer programme.

If you want your students to do laboratory work which stimulates and fosters their curiosity and creativity and gives them freedom to invent new ways of doing things, you will want to use lab guides with circumspection. You may also want more flexibility for yourself and more opportunities for change and innovation. In this case, you may like to operate a compromise system: you could produce briefing sheets as the need arises and ask students to put together their own lab guides. Or you could store the briefing material on an open access computer, where it can be updated as necessary, and indicate to students which pages they need to print off for themselves prior to each session.

If you decide to produce lab guides, in whatever form, these are some of the aspects of practical work which you could include.

•   All students should be given information about health and safety regulations in the laboratory and the control of substances hazardous to health (COSHH). This information could go into your lab guide.

•   It is useful for students to have a complete list of all the practicals which they are required to do on a course. Where students rotate round a series of practicals, the organisation of this can be explained in the guide.

•   If you have a record-keeping system for keeping track of which practicals the student has done, or if you want to introduce one, this could go into your lab guide. You should also, where appropriate, include information about how many, or which, practicals will count in the assessment of the course.

•   Any general advice about experimental procedures, report writing, technical language or mathematical and statistical methods could be included.

•   Students need instructions for each practical, though the level and amount of detail will vary according to the student group.

•   These instructions can be followed up by references to background reading.

•   You may want to set questions about the practicals for the students to answer.

•   If the practicals are so standardised that you can anticipate what will be needed, you can include proformas of various kinds: record sheets, tables, axes of graphs, report writing formats etc.

•   You may also want to give students diagrams of apparatus etc.

It's impossible to link the science lectures   39
and the practicals

Many science teachers try to make meaningful links between lectures and practicals. They either use lectures to give practicals a theoretical under-pinning or use practicals to give students an opportunity to put theory into practice. Making these links has never been easy, due to extrinsic constraints such as timetabling, and intrinsic constraints such as the differences in conceptual level between the theory and the practical: many tutors in the lectures want to present students with the latest developments in their discipline whereas the practicals are limited by lack of student expertise, and the availability of enough 'state of the art' equipment.

With increasing numbers, a bigger team of staff giving the lectures and more student groups having to do practicals in alternating sessions, it is even more difficult to ensure that the lecture and the practical complement each other.

If you no longer have the accommodation or resources or student numbers to teach your subject in an integrated way, you may want to accept the inevitable and teach it as two separate courses: theory and practice. Some significant advantages in fact accrue from this.

The science lecture
The lecture can become an arena for describing and explaining abstract theories, complex processes and new developments.

The practicals
If the practicals are separated from the lectures and you are no longer designing them to illustrate the lectures, you are free to develop new criteria. You may, for example, want to design practicals which develop students' technical and experimental skills or give them opportunities to devise their own experiments or projects. Or, in situations of financial

constraint, your priority may be to make better use of the equipment and materials available.

You can still give your practicals a theoretical underpinning by requiring students to do some related reading immediately before and/or after each practical. This reading could be in the form of specially prepared handouts or directed reading from the textbook or library books.

Timetabling
If lectures and practicals are taught as two separate courses, this allows more flexibility in the timetable.

There isn't time to supervise individual projects   **40**

The final project is the culmination of the degree course. It gives students the opportunity to work independently on a topic or issue of their choice and stimulates many of them to produce their best work. On many degrees it carries more weight than any other course element.

Individual supervision is the most expensive component of any course in terms of staff time. For many institutions, faced with increasing student numbers, it is becoming too expensive. Staff need to find more efficient ways of briefing, tutoring and monitoring their project students.

Written project briefing
There are certain pieces of information which project students need: about the parameters of the project, the procedures for supervision, the format of the report, regulations for presentation, advice on record keeping, criteria for marking etc. There is no need for supervisors to see students individually to give them this information, though. It can be printed on a handout and given to students at a general meeting of the whole year group.

Group tutorials
Staff can save supervision time and also offer students a richer experience if they hold group tutorials. These need not totally replace individual sessions; it is possible to alternate the two, or perhaps offer individual tutorials to those students who are dealing with a particularly esoteric topic or encountering special difficulties.

A crucial tutorial is that early one in which students need to explore their ideas for projects, test them out on an audience and get some feedback. This lends itself particularly well to discussion by a group. Then, once students have settled on a topic for their projects, they can be organised into groups according to their subject area. Working in a specialist group with a shared interest and expertise allows them to operate at an advanced level.

These group tutorials may need to be chaired by a tutor to start with but once students are convinced of their value they will probably want to take over the running themselves.

Self and peer monitoring
An important aspect of project supervision is the monitoring of student progress: checking that they pace themselves, meet deadlines and keep records of their work, as well as remaining cheerful and confident. Monitoring lends itself ideally to groupwork. Students can hold regular self-evaluation meetings where they submit a progress report and get feedback from their peers. This is also an aspect of the project which could very easily be assessed by the students themselves.

(For discussion of group projects, see item 47.)

Large groups can't benefit from fieldwork 41

Traditionally, field trips in higher education have consisted of small student groups receiving intensive supervision and tutoring. With very small groups it is possible for a skilful tutor to foster in the students an enquiring and reflective attitude to the fieldwork. With larger groups, however, field trips become walking lectures (or even bus tours with a commentary) and students become passive.

Field guides

Large groups of students can benefit from fieldwork if a field guide is substituted for the lecture or commentary, and briefing and other preparatory work is carried out in college beforehand: time in the field is expensive and precious and should be devoted to what can only be done in the field. (You can expect to spend at least as much time in preparation as in the field.)

Field guides have the following characteristics.

- They tell students where to go.
  They include maps, drawings, photographs and instructions which enable individual students or groups to find their way easily. Routes can be organised so that different students or groups are working in different parts of the field at the same time.

- They pose questions and invite observations which encourage students to look carefully. In this way they provide the equivalent of a detailed active tutorial.
  e.g. 'You are now walking along the boundary of the reclamation project. Stop and look downslope. What do you notice about the slope immediately below the fence? What is happening to it and why?' Such questions can be followed by spaces for students to write answers. Groups of students can share a guide and discuss answers before a rapporteur writes in a response. Questions which

they are unable to answer can be dealt with afterwards.

• They set tasks which require students to interact with their environment.
   e.g. 'Draw a detailed profile of the exposed soil. What is the character of the 50mm depth immediately below?'

• They tell a story.
   By sequencing students' observations and asking particular questions they can take students through an argument or a line of enquiry. It is possible to use this feature very deliberately to enliven subsequent debriefing. For example, students can be given one of two different guides to a site: an ecologically pessimistic guide, pointing out damage to the environment, or an ecologically optimistic guide, highlighting evidence of natural regeneration. Groups can afterwards be brought together to discuss their observations.

• They allow students or groups to work at different speeds.

• They generate comprehensive notes on which to base subsequent work.

Field guides may also contain theoretical and instructional material, but it is their interactive nature which is their distinguishing feature.

The preparation of field guides obviously takes time, and necessitates a careful examination of the site, and a feel for the kinds of observations, questions and tasks which will engage students. Once guides are prepared, however, they can enable students to undertake quite extensive fieldwork with little or no tutorial support and can be used for large numbers of students over several years with no further investment of resources. They also enable students to undertake fieldwork outside term time, or at weekends, where it will not interfere with other studies or put pressure on the goodwill of staff.

Chapter 5

Assessment

Standards are falling 42

The effects of increases in student numbers without corresponding increases in resources - overcrowding, reduced staff-student contact, deterioration in library provision etc. - are all detrimental to learning. Inevitably standards of student work are falling.

Some institutions respond to a decline in the quality of student work by statistical adjustment of marks to conceal problems. Drop-out and failure rates are performance indicators: institutions (and departments) feel they cannot afford to let the marks stand for fear of retribution. In making such adjustments, they are propping up an ineffective system by compromising on their standards.

Resist
If you are asked to collude with a rescaling of marks, it is important that you make a stand and encourage your colleagues to find more educationally sound and equitable ways of raising the level of the marks.

This chapter suggests some ways in which this can be done with large numbers.

Students' assignments are too late, too long and too illegible 43

Many tutors in higher education, while being rigorous in their criticism of the structure and content of students' assignments, have tended to be very easy going about other aspects: they have accepted late work, allowed wide variations in assignment length and generously spent time deciphering poor student handwriting.

As student numbers increase, however, staff cannot afford to be so flexible. In order to be able to cope with the marking, they need to tighten up the requirements for the submission of written work. This can be done in several ways, all of which, incidentally, will be equally helpful to students themselves if they are doing self and peer assessment. They also encourage the development of personal transferable skills.

If you plan to introduce any changes of this kind, you must of course give students full information about the new regulations, the reasons why you are making the changes, and any sanctions you plan to impose. These could be included in the course handbook so that students have plenty of notice of what to expect. And if you explain how the new requirements will help students as well as staff they will be happier to comply with them.

Firm deadlines
All or most of your students will hand in their assignments on the due date if you have firm deadlines, strict rules about extensions and sanctions for the late submission of work. This will help both you and your students to predict the demands on your time and organise your work. It is also the only way to be fair to all students.

In the long term you may even want to adopt the system which is used in many American and continental universities which is that if students miss this year's deadline, they have another chance to submit their assignment next year.

Shorter assignments

A shorter assignment is not only quicker to read and mark but also has educational benefits for the student: learning to write to a specific length by distilling ideas and presenting them succinctly is an important transferable skill.

If you want your students to write shorter assignments, you will need to specify word limits and ensure that students keep to them, by penalising assignments which are too long. You will also need to set assignment topics which can be satisfactorily covered within the word limit.

Wordprocessed assignments

Assignments which are typed are not only much quicker to read but also easier to assess comparatively.

If you want to insist on typed assignments you will need to mount word-processing courses for your students. These take about six half days and should be held at the earliest opportunity, ideally at the beginning of the students' first year. They also require the back-up of a computer room with staff on hand to help students when they get stuck.

Students soon recognise the benefits of the wordprocessor in enabling them to redraft and reorganise their assignments. Not only do they save themselves time but also they produce better work. And they can keep track of the length of their assignments more easily with a wordprocessing programme which counts words.

Wordprocessing is another important personal transferable skill. If you have facilities to help your students acquire this skill, you could make it a feature when advertising the course or writing references for your students.

It's hard to mark consistently   **44**

The more students there are on a course and the more tutors who are responsible for the assessment of the students' work, the more difficult it is for the tutors to be consistent in their marking.

One way of ensuring consistency in marking is to use objective tests (see item 45). Objective tests are not the answer, however, in whole areas of assessment where the students are being assessed on their ability to present an argument, evaluate an issue, or think creatively. In these areas, other measures are needed. Three suggestions are offered here.

Marking schemes
If the markers can agree among themselves what they are looking for in a piece of student work this will help them to mark more fairly. If in addition they can specify what constitutes an answer which merits a first, upper second, lower second etc., this will help them to classify the assignments more consistently. And clearly, if students are given this information or involved in the production of it, the standard of their work will improve.

Computer adjustments
The computer can be used to keep a check on the marking. (This is particularly easy if students' marks are kept on the computer anyway.) Comparisons, in terms of means and standard deviations, for example, can be made between different tutors on the same course, who can then be given feedback about their set of marks compared with those of their colleagues. Tutor marks can also be adjusted to eliminate bias though this is only statistically valid with large numbers.

Teaching assistants
If one person marks all the assignments, the results are likely to be more consistent. It is not, however, generally considered possible for one tutor to cope with the written work of large numbers of students, so some institutions use teaching assistants as markers. If the teaching assistant is

properly trained for the job and provided with full marking schemes, and supervised and paid adequately, this method can solve some of the problems of inconsistency between markers. It can also save staff time, though it is necessary for staff to be involved in monitoring the teaching assistant's marking. It carries with it, however, the disadvantages that the tutors can miss out on the feedback on their teaching which they normally get from reading students' assignments and the students can find it disconcerting to have one person teaching them and another person marking their work.

It's hard to mark objectively   **45**

Much of the marking of assignments in higher education is subjective. This is inevitable, particularly where students are being encouraged to explore issues and develop individual approaches and responses to their studies, though staff can guard against subjectivity to a certain extent though the use of criteria, the practice of second marking and monitoring by external examiners.

Objective tests

The only way to mark objectively is to use objective tests. These use questions of the following types.

Right/Wrong	Short Answer
Completion	True/False
Matching	Multiple Choice
Multiple Completion	Assertion/Reason
Best Answer	

The main advantage of objective tests is that, if they are well written, they are highly reliable. Reliability is particularly relevant where a team of tutors is responsible for assessment. Objective tests can also be marked quickly, especially where students indicate their answers by ticking possible alternatives as with multiple choice questions.

And they can be marked easily. This can allow either less experienced tutors (for example, post-graduates or third year undergraduates), students' peers or even computers to mark student work (see item 46).

Although objective tests are no substitute for assessment by essay, project etc., it makes sense to use them for all testing of knowledge and understanding. It is also possible to devise objective tests which involve discrimination, analysis, computation and interpretation. These are time-consuming to devise but can be re-used, if varied slightly, from year to year.

It is, however, not always necessary for tutors to devise their own multiple choice questions: many standard textbooks are nowadays accompanied by tutor guides containing banks of well designed questions.

Objective tests can be used in a variety of ways with large classes.
* Objective tests are particularly useful as one component of assessment, achieving some of the aims of assessment very economically and releasing resources to be allocated to other more demanding areas. They can, for example, replace the short-answer first sections of conventional exams.

* Objective tests can be used to focus students' attention on some basic features of the content of the course which, in a large group, might otherwise pass unnoticed.

* Objective tests can quickly provide lecturers with information on the progress of the whole class so that they can decide what to include in remedial lectures or problem sessions.

* Objective tests can be used to provide regular and frequent feedback to students. They can use this information as a self-diagnostic tool in making decisions about whether to do further work or to attend additional classes.

Fuller explanations of objective tests, and illustrative examples, can be found in *53 Interesting ways to assess your students*, in this series.

There isn't time to do all the marking   46

Computer marking is quicker than other methods. And though many types of assignment - essays, projects, reports, presentations - cannot of course be marked by the computer, many others - multiple choice questions, calculations and other problems - lend themselves to computer marking. And in some ways the computer offers a better service than the human marker, not only in terms of speed but also by providing personalised tests for the students and statistical information about student progress to the tutor.

These are some ways in which the computer can help you with your marking.

Computer marking
The computer can mark your multiple choice question tests automatically. This is done using an optical mark reader (OMR), which recognises and records responses made on pre-printed forms. Standard OMR systems use forms on which students can indicate which of five alternative answers they have selected for up to 120 multiple choice questions. Computer software is now available to interpret and collate data and print out results, which will run on most of the commonly used personal computers (PC's). Computer centres in some institutions already offer this service, or would advise on a system cheap enough for departments to purchase.

Computer questions, answers and scores
The computer can present your students with multiple choice questions on screen. Software for standard PC's is available which enables you to set up questions which students can then work on in their own time. Their answers can be scored and collated automatically and the results made accessible to the tutor.

Unique problems
The computer can be programmed to present unique problems to each

student. In numerical work it is often necessary to provide unique problems for each student in order to reduce the copying of answers. As class sizes increase, the workload involved in generating unique problems and calculating the accompanying unique answers for marking purposes can be prohibitive. The simplest way to deal with this is to have each student presented with a random sample of questions drawn from a question bank. Alternatively, user-friendly software is available for generating unique problems and solutions from algorithms provided by the tutor. A print-out is produced for each student with unique numerical values for each problem type and a second matching print-out gives the solutions.

In a refinement of this method, and using 'on screen' testing, students are free to insert their own values for each of the variables in a set of standard problems and the computer marks them as before.

Computer data
The computer can give you information on your students' progress. If the computer is marking your students' work, it can provide you with various sorts of data: you will probably want lists of marks; you may also like to know, for instance, the names of all students who failed or got less than the average mark; and some programmes will give you information on how many attempts students made before they got the answers right.

Of course, it is a simple matter for the computer to archive, update and map all the marks of all the students as the course progresses so that any trends or problems can be identified.

It's difficult to mark group projects fairly   47

As student numbers increase and resources diminish, individual student projects, with their heavy demands on equipment, library facilities and staff supervision and marking time, need to be replaced by group projects. It is clearly quicker to supervise and assess ten teams of six students than sixty individuals.

There are educational benefits too: groups achieve more than individuals, tackling more complex problems, collecting more data, and writing fuller, more sophisticated reports. And group presentations, as well as being of a higher quality, are less stressful for individual students and more entertaining and instructive for the audience.

Groupwork skills are also sought after by employers. Group project work is an ideal vehicle for the development of such skills as communication, leadership, chairing, organisation and peer tutoring.

The one problem with group projects is that of assessment: degrees and other qualifications are awarded to individuals and so students need to be assessed individually. Teachers feel that it would be difficult to allocate marks to individuals within a group and unfair to give all members of the group the same mark in case some of them did less work than others. Indeed group assessment in which everyone gets the same mark regardless of their contribution is often seen as encouraging some students not to pull their weight. There are, however, several simple mechanisms for allocating marks to individuals which overcome these problems.

Shared group mark

If your students are working in groups of six, and one group's assignment earns a mark of 50%, then you simply give the group (6 x 50)= 300 marks to divide among themselves as they see fit. The students are in the best position to know who deserves what mark.

If you think they might collude and agree to give everyone in the group the same mark despite obvious differences, you can decide that this is their responsibility rather than yours and hope that they learn from the experience. Or you can use one of the following methods to elicit different marks for different group members.

• Ask your groups, at the start of the assignment, to discuss how they plan to divide up the marks at the end, and to specify in writing what criteria they will use. This ensures that students are aware from the outset of the consequences of not pulling their weight. When you have marked and handed back the assignments, ask the group to use their own criteria to divide up the marks. This helps students to be more discriminating about one another's contributions and to overcome some of the social awkwardness of peer assessment.

• If the assignment has a number of distinct components, group members can draw up a contract specifying which components each member is responsible for. You can either mark the components separately or, putting the responsibility back on the students, ask them to assess the extent to which members fulfilled their contracts and completed their components successfully. They can be allowed to moderate your group mark up or down 5% for each member.

Peer assessment of contributions to the group assignment
Start by specifying a number of aspects of the assignment which you want students to focus on. (In the example below, the headings relate to the stages of a social science enquiry.) Give each group a mark for their assignment and then ask the students to assess the relative contribution made in each of these areas by each of the members of their group. They can moderate individual marks up or down a little. The only rule is that the average of the moderated marks must be the same as your group mark: in other words they are not allowed to mark everybody up. You can specify any aspects or criteria you like, and you may wish to specify different criteria for different assignments. You may also wish to negotiate criteria with your students or even give them responsibility for devising their own (see item 51).

132

Relative contribution to the project

Aspect of the project	*below average*		*average*		*above average*
Formulation of the problem	-2%	-1%	0%	+1%	+2%
Design of the study	-2%	-1%	0%	+1%	+2%
Collection of the data	-2%	-1%	0%	+1%	+2%
Analysis of the data	-2%	-1%	0%	+1%	+2%
Writing of theoretical section	-2%	-1%	0%	+1%	+2%
Presentation of results	-2%	-1%	0%	+1%	+2%

Group mark ....

Sum of moderated marks (-12% to +12%) ....

Individual mark ....

Viva

In just a brief viva it is possible to obtain a fair impression of an individual's contribution to a group assignment. With the assignment in front of you, ask questions such as 'What was your contribution to this section?' or 'Whose idea was this?' You can allow yourself the freedom to moderate students' marks up or down a maximum of 10% depending on the impression you obtain in the viva. It is important that students know at the outset that they will be assessed in this way as this will affect their behaviour in their group. Obviously vivas take time, but marking one substantial assignment and conducting a series of brief vivas can still be quicker than marking a series of assignments.

Project exam questions

Another way of obtaining a mark for each individual within a group is to set exam questions on the group assignment. Questions can take a variety of forms such as:

Describe how your group went about ...

If your group, instead of being asked to ..... had been asked to ....., how would you have gone about it?

Identify the strengths and weaknesses of your group's work, and explain how you would tackle a similar task differently next time.

Explain the concept of .... with reference to your group assignment.

What methods can be used to .... ? Select one of these methods to explain in detail, using your group assignment as an example.

For ways of helping students to develop groupwork skills, see item 35.

It's impossible to give students fully individualised written feedback 48

The essay is still the main type of assessment used in further and higher education. It is also one of the most time-consuming to mark because all the essays in a set are different from one another and require different feedback. With increasing numbers it is becoming impossible to give totally individualised feedback to so many students. And yet feedback is crucial to formative assessment: students need to be given information about their performance so that they can learn from the experience of writing the essay, build on their strengths and carry forward suggestions for improvement.

There are, however, ways in which tutors can standardise some common aspects of the feedback, and which allow correspondingly more time for those other aspects which differ from one essay to another. Some suggestions follow.

Standard format
If you arrange the feedback under headings, this helps you to think clearly and write succinctly and so save time. The headings can also help the students to understand the point of the feedback you are giving them. A simple set of headings is:
Some things I like about your essay.
Some suggestions for improvement.

Feedback form
You can devise a feedback form to suit your course which could specify criteria and maybe use ratings with boxes for comments. If students are involved in the production of the form or at least invited to suggest modifications to it, this will help them to take their feedback seriously and learn from it. If in addition the form is printed on NCR (No Carbon Required) paper, it will ease the task of record keeping. Two examples of such forms, one for practical reports and one for essays, are shown at the

end of this item.

Generalised feedback

Although essays are unique, the experience of the tutor marking them is that some of the feedback becomes very repetitive: particular misunderstandings, omissions or biases occur over and over. It is worthwhile drawing up a sheet of these common errors and giving copies to all students. You can also cross refer from individual students' essays to items on the sheet.

Wordprocessor

A refinement of the above suggestions is to use a wordprocessor to build up a bank of general feedback items, either from the criteria agreed with the students at the start or from the feedback form, from which you can select those which apply to individual essays. A student's personalised feedback sheet could then consist of a general comment about the way the class as a whole handled the assignment, including reference to any common errors or general problems experienced, one or two items from the bank, and a short piece of feedback addressed to the individual, together with any other information you wish to give to the class as a whole.

Audiotape recorder

Since speaking is quicker than writing, you can save time and give students more feedback if you record your comments as you read their essays. If the cost of tapes is a problem you can ask students to submit a tape with each essay.

Assignment Attachment Sheet: BSc (Psychology & Health Studies)

Name		Marker	
Date in	Date back		Mark

WRITER'S SPECIFIC REQUESTS FOR FEEDBACK

MARKER'S GENERAL VIEW OF THE WORK

RATING SCALE	Excellent	Very good	Satis-factory	Needs some more work	Needs much more work
INTRODUCTION TO THE ESSAY					
Interpretation of title and introduction	......	......	.....	......	.....
DEVELOPMENT OF THE ESSAY					
Logical development	......	......	.....	.....	.....
Insight and originality	......	......	.....	.....	.....
Subject relevance	......	......	.....	.....	.....
Use of sources	......	......	.....	.....	.....
Use of evidence	......	......	.....	.....	.....
Understanding of topic	......	......	.....	.....	.....
Constructive critical analysis	......	......	.....	.....	.....
CONCLUSION TO THE ESSAY	......	......	.....	.....	.....
OTHER FEATURES					
Presentation of references	......	......	.....	.....	.....
Legibility	......	......	.....	.....	.....
Spelling	......	......	.....	.....	.....
Grammar & Syntax	......	......	.....	.....	.....
Style	......	......	.....	.....	.....
Length	......	......	.....	.....	.....
Overall presentation	......	......	.....	.....	.....

SPECIFIC ASPECTS OF YOUR ESSAY ....that the marker likes	SPECIFIC ASPECTS OF YOUR ESSAY ....that need more work

BSc (Psychology & Health Studies) Practical Comment Sheet

Name: _____   Date submitted: _____

Practical: _____   Mark: _____

Marker: _____

Checklist of comments

TITLE (2%)

[ ] Missing   [ ] Correct   [ ] Incorrect   [ ] Vague   [ ] Too short   [ ] Too long   [ ] Incorrect, but adequate

COMMENT:

ABSTRACT (5-10%)

[ ] Needs heading 'abstract' or 'summary'   [ ] Section missing [ ] Too short   [ ] Too long (200w)   [ ] Unclear

[ ] Wrongly placed, move to beginning [ ] Omits hypothesis   [ ] Omits aim/design/procedure/results   [ ] Conclusion

[ ] Clear   [ ] Succinct   [ ] Material which is here belongs elsewhere

COMMENT:

INTRODUCTION (10-20%)

[ ] Parts missing   [ ] Heading missing   [ ] Too short (min. 300w) [ ] Too long (max. 1,000w)   [ ] About right length

[ ] Follows handout too closely   [ ] Rambling & unfocussed   [ ] Does not incorporate statement of hypothesis

[ ] Rationale missing   [ ] Rationale for study missing   [ ] Does not review previous empirical findings

[ ] Omits relevant readings [ ] Well argued   [ ] Does not consider appropriate theories [ ] Material included here belongs elsewhere

[ ] Shows set reading has been done   [ ] Inappropriate use of references   [ ] States hypotheses if appropriate

COMMENT:

METHOD (30-40%)

[ ] The entire section is missing   [ ] Should be subdivided as below:

SUBJECTS

[ ] Number?   [ ] Groups?   [ ] Sex?   [ ] Age?   [ ] Naive to purposes of study   [ ] Method of sampling

MATERIALS/APPARATUS

[ ] Section missing [ ] Not enough detail   [ ] Too much detail[ ] Needs diagram

DESIGN

[ ] Section missing   [ ] Control(s)?   [ ] Balancing?   [ ] Randomisation?   [ ] Inappropriate

PROCEDURE

[ ] Section missing   [ ] Instructions to subjects   [ ] Details missing   [ ] Too detailed

[ ] Whole section clear and detailed   [ ] Possible to replicate on basis of description

COMMENT:

RESULTS (20-30%) *(Quantitative analysis)*

TABLES

[ ] Missing   [ ] Summary table needed   [ ] No numbers/titles on tables   [ ] Tables don't show what you've found

[ ] Calculations/Raw data go into Appendix   [ ] Untidy   [ ] Neat

FIGURES/GRAPHS

[ ] Missing   [ ] Axes need labelling   [ ] Key to symbols?   [ ] Untidy

[ ] Neat   [ ] No number/titles on figures (e.g. Figure 1: Graph of ....)

DESCRIPTION OF DATA

[ ] Missing   [ ] Too short   [ ] Good length   [ ] Put some of this into Discussion

STATISTICS

[ ] All the tests described not done   [ ] Link this with a table/result   [ ] Arithmetic errors   [ ] Data well presented

[ ] Verbal description clear & precise   [ ] Understands significance levels

COMMENT:

DISCUSSION (20-30%) *(Quantitative analysis)*

[ ] Missing   [ ] Too short   [ ] Too long   [ ] Not enough evidence or reading   [ ] Mention problems with design/procedure

[ ] Satisfactory   [ ] Well-argued   [ ] Well organised   [ ] Some material would be better in the intro   [ ] Contains new, interesting points

[ ] Answers research question   [ ] Recommend replication with more rigour   [ ] Recommend replication with extension

[ ] Results are repeated but implications are missing   [ ] Shows implications of statistically significant differences

COMMENT:

REFERENCES (5%)

[ ] Some refs incomplete (Min. information is (a) first author; (b) title of article or book; (c) title of journal).

[ ] Some refs not detailed here   [ ] Some refs inaccurate   [ ] Section missing [ ] Satisfactory

COMMENT:

PRESENTATION (1-5%)

[ ] Clean & neat   [ ] Messy and difficult to decipher

COMMENT:

GENERAL

[ ] Poor   [ ] Fair   [ ] Good   [ ] Very good   [ ] Excellent   [ ] Too brief overall

[ ] Too hurriedly written   [ ] Poor spelling   [ ] Report not set out in formal order   [ ] Poor grammar   [ ] Untidy

[ ] Arguments difficult to follow   [ ] Too long (Condense argument)   [ ] Overall presentation good

[ ] Demonstrates reading beyond given references and extra marks awarded for this   [ ] Does not understand the point of the practical

COMMENT:

Tutors can't do all the marking unaided   4

If students mark their own and one another's work, this not only saves staff time but also helps the students to acquire the skills of criticism and self-criticism. Many teachers, however, are nervous about handing over the whole of the assessment to students: they feel it would be a dereliction of duty on their part and they are aware of the many pitfalls for students which surround self and peer assessment.

If you would like to be able to benefit your students and yourself by introducing some aspects of self and peer assessment but without giving up the ultimate responsibility for grading, you can arrange for your students to give one another feedback but not marks. Two ways of doing this are described here.

The students add to the tutor's feedback
The tutor marks the essays, writing on them as much feedback as time allows. When the essays are returned to the group, students are invited to give one another supplementary feedback. They can do this in pairs, reading each other's essays and then adding to the tutor's feedback. Or, if they would like feedback from more than one person, and if they are willing to spend the time required for this, they can do a group feedback exercise. In this exercise, students put their essays together on a table and then pick one out, read it and write comments on it. When they have finished with the first, they replace it and pick out a second and then a third, and so on. If you operate a system of anonymous marking, this will help students in the group exercise not to feel too exposed in presenting their essays for comment.

The tutor adds to the students' feedback
Instead of handing in their essays to the tutor after finishing them, students first write a critique of their own work and then get written feedback from other students in the group. (This can be organised as described above.) The essays are then handed in with this self and peer evaluation appended.

ne tutor writes a brief response to the evaluation, adds any points which seem to be missing, and decides on the grades. This is an efficient way of marking because allocating grades is the quickest part of the process and students' self and peer evaluation is generally quite adequate - and improves with practice.

If you want to try full-scale self and peer assessment, see item 52. (You can of course mix peer and tutor assessment on your course.)

It's impossible to give students one-to-one tutorials

The one-to-one tutorial is the ideal situation in which to give your students live feedback on their written work and to enter into a dialogue with them about their studies. It has been a staple of higher education for generations. But once a class grows beyond a certain size, individual tutorials become an impossibility.

There are, however, some ways of working with marked assignments in the whole group which carry with them some of the benefits of the individual tutorial. For these to work well, you need to make a clear statement to your students of the limitations which have been imposed upon you, as well as a rationale for the use of each method.

Model assignment

Many students go through their whole course without ever seeing a piece of written work which is better than their own. (And some never see another student's work at all.) If you give them a photocopy of a first class assignment they should be able to judge for themselves some ways in which their own work is falling short and get a better sense of what they are aiming for next time. This will be more likely if you discuss with them the features of the model assignment which make it good. The assignment could be the best one produced by that group or, preferably, one from a previous year but either way you should obtain the permission of the student concerned.

A risk with using a model assignment is that students will think that there is only one way to write well. And some of them may feel intimidated by work which is much better than theirs. It is important that you address these issues in your discussion with them.

Mediocre assignment

Students will often feel happier discussing a mediocre assignment than a model one, especially if they are invited to suggest improvements. You could give them photocopies of the assignment and say 'This assignment got 55%. How could it have been better?' or 'How could it have got a higher mark?'

In a large class you could ask students to discuss the assignment in sub-groups and report on their conclusions in a plenary session. Or you could organise the discussion in a pyramid (see item 31). The stages of the pyramid could be, for example,

Stage 1   Students individually read the assignment and make notes (10 minutes).

Stage 2   Students in pairs discuss the assignment (10 minutes).

Stage 3   Students in groups of four draw up check lists of characteristics of a good assignment (20 minutes).

However you organise the discussion, it is essential that students have the opportunity to reflect on what they have learned from it and apply it to their own assignments. This means setting aside time at the end for them to re-read their assignments with the discussion in mind.

In the case of a mediocre assignment, it is clearly important to use anonymously the work of a past student so that members of the group can feel free to say whatever they like in the discussion. You can of course reuse photocopies from year to year if you ask students not to write on them.

Comparing assignments

Students who have difficulty commenting on one assignment will probably find it easier to make a comparison between two assignments which illustrate good and mediocre technique or alternatively are good or mediocre in different ways. A comparative exercise of this kind could also help to prepare a group for the activity of self and peer assessment.

Role play tutorial

An important feature of the one-to-one tutorial is the opportunity it gives the student to talk about the assignment to a tutor who has read it and is willing to discuss it supportively. Even if the tutor no longer has the time for such tutorials, the role can still be adopted by the students themselves, working in pairs and taking turns as 'student' and 'tutor' for twenty minutes each.

To organise this, you first ask the students to read one another's essay in pairs. Then you need to give them a full explanation of the process. You could say 'The reason we're doing this is so that you can get the kind of support and feedback you would like from a tutorial. So when it's your turn to be student, try to be very clear about what you want from your partner, who will be taking the role of tutor. For example you may want feedback which could be general or specific, positive or negative, or mixed. Or you may want to discuss with your partner the difficulties of writing the assignment. Or you may simply want your partner to listen while you talk about what you've written. And when it's your turn to play the role of tutor, try to give your partner exactly the kind of support which he or she asks for. I'm available for consultation if anyone wants me'.

When students have finished the 'tutorials', it is a good idea to bring the whole group back together again to give them the chance to deal with any problems or queries. It is also helpful if you make them the offer of supplementary tutorials with you, perhaps during a short 'surgery' period later on. This should not be very onerous because if the exercise has been successful the number coming forward will be quite small.

Self and peer assessment may be a solution but students can't do it without training

Many tutors would like their students to do self and peer assessment but are worried that the results will be unreliable. It is true that inexperienced students are often excessively harsh or excessively lenient on themselves and others. They can also be unsophisticated in the range of criteria they use and may allow themselves to be swayed by superficial features such as neatness.

But experienced students can mark as reliably as a second marker who is a tutor, and they can predict their own marks with great accuracy. Once students are experienced, they will not only save a great deal of your time if they assess their own work but they will also learn more.

If the benefits of self and peer assessment are to be exploited to help tutors cope with large classes, then students' judgment needs to be developed. This can be done by using a selection of the following mechanisms before allowing students' own grades to count towards their final result.

Advance warning
It is important to tell students at the beginning of the year about self and peer assessment and to explain to them why, how and when they will be doing it. You can also reassure them that you will give them all the support and training they need.

Staff-generated criteria
Students need full, explicit and unambiguous information about the criteria which their tutors use to allocate marks. It can also be helpful to spell out for them the distinguishing features of first class, average and poor answers. And to list practices which should be avoided at all costs.

Student-generated criteria
Alternatively, you can help students to generate their own criteria by using

...ne following exercise.

a   Ask students to choose one of the assessment questions and spend 10 minutes writing on that topic. Warn them that they will be asked to read out what they have written to a small group of fellow students.

b   Get students to form groups of four. Ask them in each group to take on the roles of reader, listeners (two students) and observer, and to proceed as follows.

> The reader reads out what he or she has written.
> The two listeners listen and give feedback to the reader.
> The observer notes down the criteria which the feedback seems to be based on.

The groups of four rotate roles until everyone has played the part of reader, listener (twice) and observer. Allow 10 minutes for each person.

c   Ask students to contribute criteria from the list they made as observer. Put these together into a list on the board. A little grouping and collapsing together of items may be necessary at this stage.

d   If staff criteria have been specified for the course, you can compare the student list with the staff's. Both groups may be able to learn something from this comparison.

Marking schemes

In scientific and technical subjects marks are often allocated in a structured way, according to a strict marking scheme. If you use such a scheme in your subject area you can help students in their self and peer assessment by giving them copies of it to work with. Some schemes are so simple and unambiguous that students quickly learn to use them reliably. Class sessions can be used, even with very large student numbers, to redistribute students' completed work, have it peer marked, and discuss model answers, without much effort on the tutor's part.

If you do not normally use such a scheme, students can find it ve
illuminating if you devise one, in consultation with them, and ask them t
use it to mark their own and one another's work. Students who have
repeatedly been told of the importance of, for example, properly labelled
graphs can take this criterion to heart for the first time when they start
subtracting and losing marks.

Marking exercises

Three kinds of marking exercise are described in item 50: *model assignment, mediocre assignment* and *comparing assignments*. These exercises
can be used to develop students' judgment in preparation for self and peer
assessment activities.

Self-assessment sheets

From the start you can encourage students to be reflective about the quality
of their work by asking them to attach a self-assessment sheet to their
assignments when they submit them. Early self-assessment sheets can
pose simple open-ended questions such as:

What are the main strengths of this piece of work?
What would you need to do to improve it?
What aspects of it would you like feedback on?

As students become more sophisticated they can be asked tougher
questions such as:

What are the main weaknesses of this piece of work?
Which criteria does it meet, and which does it not meet?
What comments will the tutor probably make on it?

Next, students can be asked to comment on the grading:

What grade do you think this piece of work will get?
Why does it deserve that grade?
What would you have to do to earn a higher grade?

You can give students feedback not just on the assignment itself, but also
on the quality of their self-assessment.

Negotiated marks

After some experience of making judgements about the grades they expect to get, and comparing these with the grades they actually get, students can be asked to propose grades for themselves. You can agree to accept these grades provided they are very close to your own. If there is a discrepancy (and by this time it will be most common for students to give themselves too low a grade) then you can have a very brief meeting to negotiate though you can retain your right to determine the grade in the event of an unresolved disagreement. Through this process students will become better at calibrating their self-assessment judgements and recognising why discrepancies occur.

Self assessment

When you are satisfied that students have developed the skills of self assessment and that the discrepancies between their grades and yours are few, or result from perfectly valid differences of perspective, you may feel confident enough to allow students' self-assigned grades to stand, for an agreed proportion of the assessed work. You will still need to give students the opportunity to check their grades with one another or with you when they are unsure. And you will need to monitor the grades by a process of comparison and spot checks.

Peer assessment

Only after students have been through some of the above stages is it wise to allow them to assess one another without any intervention or moderation on your part. See item 52 for a description of the process.

Self and peer assessment may be a solution but it's difficult to organise

As well as reducing the burden of marking for staff, self and peer assessment offers a number of benefits to students: in general those of increased confidence and autonomy and in particular the development of the skills of criticism and self criticism.

Organising a self and peer assessment session

The previous item suggests ways of preparing students for self and peer assessment. This item illustrates the process by describing one way of organising such a session. The details of this description are important: they are designed to help the session to run smoothly and without too much stress for students or staff.

The session takes three hours and requires the use of an extra classroom if possible.

a   Before students write their assignments you should agree with them a set of assessment criteria. These criteria can form the basis for the group's marking sheet. Examples of such marking sheets are shown at the end of this item.

b   Make enough copies of the marking sheet for students to have several copies each. Give them one copy each at this stage and ask them to use it to write a self assessment when they have done the assignment.

c   On the due date, ask students to hand in, together with their assignments, an envelope with their name on it - or their number if assessment is to be anonymous - containing the self assessment. (You may want to leave a week between the due date and the assessment session so that students can distance themselves from their assignments and those with extensions can submit their work in time for the session.)

d   At the start of the session, ask students to form two groups and to stack their assignments, complete with envelopes, in two piles, one for each group. Give each group half the marking sheets. One group then goes into the extra classroom, taking with them a stack of marking sheets and the other group's assignments. (This ensures that self assessment is separated from peer assessment.)

e   Students spend the first half hour passing round the assignments in their group, looking through them and gaining a general impression of the work.

f   After half an hour, they start marking. They each read one assignment, fill in one of the marking sheets and then put the sheet in the envelope attached to the assignment. As they mark one they return it to the pile and take another, continuing with further marking until the time is up.

g   Half an hour before the end of the session, ask them to stop marking and start making decisions. Tell them that both groups need to agree a mark for all the assignments in their room. They can organise this in any way they like. For example, they could average the marks on the mark sheets for each assignment. Or they could set aside all the assignments which are easy to agree and discuss the difficult ones, including those where there is a noticeable discrepancy in the marks. Finally they should write on each envelope the agreed mark for the assignment. (If they really cannot agree on any of the assignments - maybe because the student has written about something outside their experience - they should write a note on the envelope explaining their disparate views, for moderation by the tutor.) The envelope and its contents are ultimately returned to the writer of the assignment.

Note:
The session works best with a group of 20 -30 students (and sub-groups of 10-15) using separate classrooms. With larger groups the session can still be run but without the discussion and with an arithmetical averaging of the grades awarded.

Example 1
(BEd Science Education)
Peer Assessed Project in Nutrition **H612a**

The project will be peer assessed on 3 December.
Non-attendance on this date will mean that your project is not marked.
We have agreed the following criteria.

Presentation
(1)	.....	Is it presented on time?
(3)	.....	Is it passable prose?
(3)	.....	Is it a pleasure to read?
(3)	.....	Is it legible, well laid out and well designed?

Approach
(5)	.....	Is the level suitable for the audience?
(5)	.....	Does it challenge the reader?
(5)	.....	Does it cover the range and scope that the title suggests?
(5)	.....	Does it extend the reader into new areas of concern?

Content & Comment
With reference to the learning objectives of *know, understand, apply, analyse,*
synthesise and *evaluate* does it:

(10)	.....	select from the material available that which is relevant?
(10)	.....	identify strengths and weaknesses in the data/material?
(10)	.....	attempt unbiased criticism of the material?
(10)	.....	bring to the reader's attention other evidence to support or discredit these criticisms?
(10)	.....	give adequate information (& references for same) to enable the reader to form her or his own judgements?
(10)	.....	summarise the information and comments to give the reader some guidance?
(10)	.....	Spare
(100)	.....	

Example 2

BA in Literary Studies (LS8)

CREATIVE WRITING: SELF AND PEER ASSESSMENT

Atmosphere: power
                sensory clarity
                natural
                contrived
Clarity
Contrast
Do you gerrit?
Energy & pace
Enjoyment (from)
Flow
Form
Identification (with)

Imagination (& sparking off
    imagination in reader)
Interest
Originality
Point of view
Structure
Style: imagery
      rhythm
      description
      voice
Use of language
Vocabulary

***   These are criteria drawn up by the group on 30 May. You can use them as a checklist or starting point if you want, though clearly they will not all apply to every piece of work.

***   Sign your name if you want to.

***   Suggest a mark.

Some courses will have to return to the three-hour exam

The benefits of assessment by coursework are well known. Writing coursework assignments is less stressful for students than sitting exams and more helpful to learning: as well as receiving feedback and guidance as they go along, students develop the skills of researching a topic, constructing an argument and reflecting on ideas.

With very large groups, however, the marking of coursework becomes unmanageable. Suggestions of ways of sharing the marking with the students themselves are provided earlier in this chapter but if you are not able or not willing to enlist the help of your students, maybe things will get so difficult that you will be obliged to return to the three-hour exam.

If you find yourself in this position, you may like to remember that some of the benefits of coursework can be retained if you design the exam with these in mind. (This also applies in situations where the three-hour exam is required by an outside body if students are to gain professional accreditation.)

Mock exams
Set mock exams during the year and discuss them in class. This gives students some feedback and guidance and also makes the exam itself less stressful.

Questions which test students' understanding
Set questions which test students' understanding, rather than those which merely test their memory.

Questions which test students' thinking
Set questions which oblige students to think: textual analysis, data interpretation, problem solving.

ewer questions
Set fewer questions on the exam paper. Students then have more time to reflect on their answers and produce better work.

Practical work exam
You can set questions on practical work, project work or any other major learning activities which you want students to take seriously.

Research exam
You can even set an exam which depends on research. Ask students to explore a range of topics in preparation for the exam and set questions which require them to use the material which they have researched.

Index